The Power of Practice-Based Literacy Research

Accessible and inviting, this book showcases how teachers and literacy coaches can use research as a tool to teach literacy effectively and with intention. Sailors and Hoffman invite literacy specialists and practicing and preservice teachers into a conversation about how they can use research as means for professional learning, mentorship, and empowerment.

Chapters feature a wealth of tools, examples, and strategies that make key concepts in literacy research refreshing and practical. This book invites the reader to pause and reflect on the practical knowledge through special features in the book and available online as eResources, including:

- "Points to Consider" boxes to encourage reflection and deeper thinking
- "Pause and Reflect" boxes to give the reader space to apply concepts to their own work as practice-based researchers
- eResources with recommended readings and "Meet the Teacher" exemplars of teachers' stories to provoke further reflection, available on the book's webpage: www.routledge.com/9780367177607

Perfect for literacy specialists, coaches and consultants in literacy, ELA/literacy teachers, as well as preservice teachers, this book is a comprehensive and engaging guide to using research as a means to transform classrooms.

Misty Sailors is a professor of language and literacy studies and Chair of the Department of Teacher Education and Administration at the University of North Texas, USA.

James V. Hoffman is a professor of language and literacy studies and the Meadows Chair for Excellence in Education in the Department of Teacher Education and Administration at the University of North Texas, USA.

The Power of Practice-Based Literacy Research

A Tool for Teachers

Misty Sailors and James V. Hoffman

Routledge
Taylor & Francis Group

NEW YORK AND LONDON

First published 2020
by Routledge
52 Vanderbilt Avenue, New York, NY 10017

and by Routledge
2 Park Square, Milton Park, Abingdon, Oxon, OX14 4RN

Routledge is an imprint of the Taylor & Francis Group, an informa business

Library of Congress Cataloging-in-Publication Data
A catalog record for this title has been requested

ISBN: 978-0-367-17757-7 (hbk)
ISBN: 978-0-367-17760-7 (pbk)
ISBN: 978-0-429-05757-1 (ebk)

Typeset in Bembo
by Apex CoVantage, LLC

Visit the eResources: www.routledge.com/9780367177607

Contents

Figures

Figures

eResources

We have included with this book two different types of appendices. They are availalbe as electronic files that can be downloaded for classroom use. You can access these downloads by visiting the book product page on our website: www.routledge.com/9780367177607. Then click on the tab that says "eResources," and select the files. They will begin downloading to your computer.

- The first, Meet the Teacher, is a set of snapshots, videos, and artifacts that represent several teachers with whom we've worked on practice-based research studies. The set of artifacts can serve to support your thinking as you move through the book, as conversation starters with others, and for reflection.
- The second, the Reading Extensions, are sets of readings that further illustrate and explain the concepts we introduce in each of the chapters.

About the Authors

This book is a collaborative effort brought about by our (Misty and Jim) shared experiences, goals, and commitments. It represents our work with beginning and in-serving teachers in our local contexts as well as those teachers with whom we've worked internationally. We were inspired to write this book by beginning teachers, classroom teachers, and reading specialists at our previous institutions. They are both excited about the energy they have found at their current institution and the goals and dedication of their colleagues there to improve the educational experiences of children and youth.

Misty Sailors is a professor of language and literacy studies and Chair of the Department of Teacher Education and Administration at the University of North Texas. Misty is celebrating her 30th year as an educator, including her nine years as a first-grade teacher, her time as a reading specialist and literacy coach, and her time at the University of Texas at San Antonio.

James V. Hoffman is a professor of language and literacy studies in the Department of Teacher Education and Administration at the University of North Texas. Jim is celebrating his 50th year in education, including his years as a 1st/2nd grade teacher, his time as a reading specialist, and his time at the University of Texas at Austin.

Preface

We are pleased that you have chosen to engage with us in this book, "The Power of Practice-Based Literacy Research: A Tool for Teachers." Our aim is to engage you, our reader, in what we call practice-based research. You may have come to this book from a variety of spaces—you might be enrolled in a university course and your capstone experience may be a practice-based research project. You may be a classroom teacher who is interested in formalizing the inquiry that you do on a regular basis. You may be a literacy coach who is hoping to engage with the teachers in your coaching circle in more authentic ways. You might be an instructional leader of a school and are hoping to bring value to the ways in which you are already supporting teacher inquiry in your school. Or, the title of the book may have interested you. Regardless, we are excited to be in this space with you and hope you see this space with us as a place of dialogue about disrupting the commonplace in literacy teaching and learning and in literacy research.

We see ourselves with you on this journey toward transforming literacy instruction. In many ways, this book was a space where we could wrap our heads around and explicate what we mean by practice-based research. In our own practices as teachers, teacher educators, and educational researchers, we have engaged in forms of practice-based research. In so many ways, that research was the basis of transformation in what we do and how we think about what we do as teachers and teacher educators. We hope that the conversations we have with you in this book create spaces in your own thinking and doing that will lead to transformation in your practice as a literacy teacher. And, we hope that the conversations we have with you spill out of the pages of the book and into the everyday conversations you have with your colleagues in the many contexts in which you find yourself.

This journey toward transformation is directed across several goals that will often intersect and interact. Our first goal is to engage with you in the use of research as a tool for becoming more intentional and more effective in your literacy teaching practices. In so many ways, traditional research has been done *on* teachers rather than *with* teachers. It is our goal to ask you to think with us about the research *in* teaching rather than research *on* teaching. In doing so, we disrupt those traditional notions of whose research "counts" and move into spaces where research that is grounded in classroom spaces (conducted by those who operate inside those spaces) is recognized to be as valuable as traditional research. In order to create those spaces, we'll share some tools with you that have been used by teachers with whom we've worked. We'll ask you to play around with these tools, modify them to meet your needs, and talk about them with your colleagues.

Our second goal is to discover ways in which these expanding sets of research tools can be used to disrupt the commonplace that is typical literacy instruction today. Throughout, we'll ask you to consider questions such as these: What instructional practices do I engage in that maintain the status quo? Are there practices that continue to "other" children and youth? How can I radically shift what I do and engage in a more critical stance in my instruction?

Our third goal is to engage you in an envisioned community of practice where we, as a collective, come to grow our practices to better serve young people and their communities in ways that foster societal change. To that end, we are cognizant of the language we use in this book—we have taken a conversational stance with you, our reader, inviting you into our shared space, intentions, and goals. We value you—as a teacher and a researcher—and use the space in this book to take a political stance toward teachers as researchers within the educational community of research practice.

We presume that we (inclusive of you, our reader, and the two of us) are at different points on this journey in terms of our experiences with research and teaching. What we share is the commitment to becoming more than what we are, and that becoming more requires that we draw on each other as resources—intellectually, culturally, emotionally, linguistically, politically, and spiritually.

This brings us to our fourth goal, which advocates for the importance of research as a pedagogical stance in our work with preservice teachers, in-service teachers, and the children in their presence. We believe not only that we as teachers and teacher educators should be engaged as researchers, both in our professional development and in our daily routines in our classrooms, but also that the children and young people in our classrooms should be nurtured into their role as researchers of their own worlds through the curriculum and instructional support of their teachers. Some might advise to take one step at a time. We respond by saying that to move forward on any of these four goals without engaging in the others is to lose the synergy of practice as a holistic philosophy for change. Research must be used to

- transform our practices,
- transform our contexts, and
- transform the lives of the children, youth, and communities with whom we work.

Drawing upon histories of teacher research, action research, design-development research, and transformative research, we engage you in an imagined "we" in a type of teaching and learning that fosters professional learning and social change.

Most often, research is positioned as something done for teachers by those who possess skills that are beyond the grasp of those who teach. We write as teachers for teachers. We write as people who are "unfinished" and "becoming" as humans (Horton & Freire, 1990). In this book, we demystify literacy research and invite you to take up research as essential to your practice. We hope to engage you in research *about* teaching, rather than research *on* teaching.

Warmly,
Misty and Jim

Reference

Horton, M., & Freire, P. (1990). *We make the road by walking: Conversations on education and social change.* Philadelphia, PA: Temple University Press.

Acknowledgments

We would like to recognize the many teachers who have contributed individually and collectively to our thinking as we planned and wrote this book. We appreciated your patience as we were working our way through and explicating our understanding of practice-based research. The work you did in your classrooms with your young people (and other teachers) deepened our insight into what it means to be a teacher engaged in practice-based research. We learned how to do practice-based research with you; we are humbled by your courageousness.

We also want to acknowledge the teachers who allowed us to dig deeper into their practice-based research projects as we designed and wrote this book. To the five English Language Arts and Reading teachers, Sara Dominguez, Evangelina Muniz, Amanda Rodriguez, Sue Anne Umpierre, Ellen Webber, and Amanda White, we remain appreciative of your dedication and commitment to teaching and how you think about your role as literacy teachers in the presence of young people and other teachers. We are forever humbled by your presence as classroom teachers and teacher educators.

To the three (then) beginning teachers (who are now first year teachers), Sarah Vivano, Iris Treinies, and Theresa Nguyen, we remain humbled by your passion for what you do, how engaged you are with your work, and the compassion and dedication you bring to our profession. We are elated you decided to be teachers. We would like to also acknowledge Catherine Lammert, Anne Daly, and Vickie Godfrey—your presentation of Sarah's work, Iris' work, and Theresa's work moved our thinking about practice-based research forward. We also deeply appreciate the role you played in supporting Sarah, Iris, and Theresa throughout their teacher preparation program.

Finally, we'd like to give a shout-out to Hazel—your snail mail and text messages keep us on our feet, both as your grandparents and as literacy teachers. We love watching you grow in how you present yourself via text.

Introduction

We write this book at a time in education fraught with urgency. Increasingly, teachers are being positioned as technicians who are trained to do things in highly prescribed terms. Teachers are not regarded as professionals who take on the responsibility for significant decision-making in their classrooms regarding curriculum and instruction. Fidelity, alignment, and accountability have become central discourses in the institutional context for teaching—replacing innovation, responsiveness, and responsibility as core dispositions for success as a teacher. Increasingly, research is being used as a tool that narrows rather than expands our thinking about teaching practices. The positioning of research as the source of "best practices" perpetuates the illusion that quality teaching is defined as or can be enacted through a particular curriculum or set of teaching behaviors.

We also write at a time when schools continue to mirror the inequities that exist in our society. In fact, in many cases, schools are used as tools to continue to oppress people who have historically been marginalized. The more reform efforts attempt to narrow "gaps" in educational achievement, the greater the disparities become and the more often differences are framed as deficits. We believe education, especially literacy, should be seen as a human right and a way of eliminating the education debt owed to so many children and youth (Ladson-Billings, 2006). Education must become more than preparation to "fit in" but preparation for us to challenge the structural inequities in our society and fulfill the goals of access and opportunity for all. And, those challenges can only be met and overcome by teachers who work from a space of radical transformation—of themselves, their classrooms, and how they interact with children and youth in their classrooms. We believe practice-based literacy research (that which this book is about) might be one way to center radical transformation of classroom spaces. Our stance in this book is one of a journey—a journey that we're taking with you as we move through this book, together. We organize this section by walking with you through a brief explication of some key ideas that shape the approach we take in this book: teaching as a practice, teaching with a radical imagination, and research to transform teaching.

Teaching as a Practice

Over the past three decades, a new understanding of literacy and teaching has gained momentum. The cognitive revolution that marked the change in thinking away from behaviorism is now being challenged by what is called the *practice turn*. Practice focuses not only on what we do as teachers—as literate beings in the world—but also on how we make meaning and learn through these practices. Educators, as professionals, are aligned with medical doctors and attorneys in the ways in which we practice in service to others. We are not talking about practice teaching as in getting ready to teach; rather, we are talking about the practice *of* teaching, in similar ways to how a physician practices medicine and an attorney practices law. That is, teachers, like doctors and lawyers, start their professional lives with a set of understandings, knowledge, beliefs, and dispositions, and through their everyday routines, rituals, habits, and ongoing professional learning, they refine their understandings, knowledge, beliefs, and dispositions.

The practice turn in literacy teaching has shifted focus away from the "inside-the-head" processes of teachers toward what teachers do, think, value, and embody; toward the identities teachers take on; and toward the ways teachers engage in various literacy practices with other teachers, with children and youth, with their campus and district leaders, and with the community of their school. This same practice turn is unfolding in research. While many aspects of educational research continue to embody a traditional stance toward research in classrooms (e.g., research is conducted in order to contribute to a knowledge base), many educational researchers, including many literacy researchers, have rethought what it means to do research and are operating from a social practice (oftentimes, critical) perspective. From this perspective, research must be intentional, improve people's lives, and be transformative in nature. To that end, researchers would convoke the radical imagination of the people with whom they work and their research would, in conjunction with the people with whom they are working, lead to a more just society (Haiven & Khasnabish, 2017). This turn toward practice puts a whole new perspective on research, the role of researchers in social change, and the inclusion of teachers as active and engaged educational researchers rather than just consumers of research.

Teaching With a Radical Imagination

It would be somewhat unusual to come across a standard for quality research that addresses imagination, let alone radical imagination. However, imagination is central to rethinking literacy research, what counts for research, and who is "allowed" to be called a researcher.

You probably have talked to children about using their imagination. Imagination is an important part of childhood development. But what exactly is that which we call our imagination? Our imagination is more than just our "mind's eye." It is an integral part of what it means to be human and a "completely essential condition for all human mental activity" (Vygotsky, 2004, p. 17). Likewise, Dewey (1986) recognized that "all possibilities reach us through the imagination" (p. 30). Often, people only think and talk about imagination in relation to children, especially young children. There's no reason to believe that adults do not have or do not use their imagination—we do! The only difference between our imagination and that of children is the difference in the tools we use in order to activate our imagination.

The radical imagination was a concept introduced by a French-Greek philosopher, Cornelius Castoriadis (1997). He defined the radical imagination as the ability to critically interrogate our thoughts and actions as they relate to our communities and societies. Because our society is not "given" to us by previous generations (we are participating in the construction of our society as we breathe each day), we have the ability to challenge the very notions that are oftentimes taken for granted (e.g., "It's always been that way"). In other words, it is through the use of our radical imagination, or the critical interrogation of our thoughts and actions, that we can question the very fabric of ourselves and our society, including the norms, morals, beliefs, values, and practices that drive our very existence. Thus, our radical imagination is the ability to imagine the world, life, and social institutions not as they are but as they might otherwise be (Haiven & Khasnabish, 2017). And, because our classrooms are microcosms of our larger society, we can practice this critical interrogation with the young people in our learning spaces, thus preparing them for a lifelong practice of engaging in their radical imagination.

Research That Transforms

Some argue that research is a neutral and objective type of inquiry and that passion for change (e.g., advocacy) has no place in research and should be avoided at all costs. We disagree with this view. Research, like so many other activities in our professional lives, is political. Our interests are in research as a tool for the transformation of conditions in education that are currently limiting human potential and access to resources that might improve the human condition, especially for people who have been minoritized, oppressed, and historically pushed to the margins of society. As such, we believe that research has the potential to both reveal and address issues of social inequity and justice. As educational researchers, our consciousness around these goals and dispositions demands that we pay particular attention to and be particularly careful and transparent in the ways in which we pose questions, gather data, interpret findings, and make claims about the significance of our work. It also requires that we constantly interrogate ourselves concerning the role of the people with whom we engage in our research and our relationship with them. Thus, a "research to transform" agenda is overtly political. And, a transformative research agenda reflects a moral commitment not only to the improvement of our practices as literacy professionals but also to a critical examination of institutional constraints that prevent the human development of the children, young people, early career teachers, and in-the-field teachers with whom we work.

Teaching, Research, and the Radical Imagination

Throughout this book (and your work as a researcher), we will ask you to come back into touch with your imagination, specifically your radical imagination. We will convoke your radical imagination and the role you play in a reimagined life, world, and social institutions through research. We hope you see this as a way of finding your radical imagination, reengaging with it, or simply growing it, depending on where you are in the process of your awareness and use of your radical imagination. Too often, research simply takes us further and further into rabbit holes of "significance" that might be interesting at some very narrow level. However, that kind of research (Does X work? Under what conditions does X work?) hardly scratches the surface of the daily successes and challenges for children and youth today. What, on the other hand, if we changed the requirement and standard of excellence for research that privileges radical imagination in what is studied? We will ask you to consider convoking the same radical imagination in the children and young people you teach as part of your research (Sailors, 2019).

Tools and Contexts

We presume that you are a teacher and are engaged in classrooms working with children, young people, and maybe even adult learners. We make no assumptions regarding your experience (undergraduate, beginning, seasoned). We make no assumptions around the "level" of people you teach (early childhood, elementary, junior high, secondary, undergraduates, graduates). The work of research spans all of these. And, while we make no assumptions about the disciplinary area(s) that you teach, our work has largely focused on language and literacy. To that end, we have built into this book several tools that may be useful to you on your journey into research.

First, you might revel in the writing space of a notebook. Second, systematizing your daily inquiry and framing it as research brings you into a community of practice. A local community (e.g., a class, a peer, a mentor, a study group) will be of tremendous value as you grow your research practices. Third, we presume that your research work will unfold in the context of a group of learners. You may be the teacher of record. You may be the instructor in a course. You may be a member of an instructional team. These instructional settings that exist inside of institutional structures may well become the focus for study. Finally, much of the work we will do through this book will engage you with the resources available on the Internet, including traditional sources of information (e.g., journal articles) and more immediate forms of knowledge (e.g., blogs of other researchers and social media).

Ethical and Legal Issues

How do you regard the people in your research work? Are you trusted? What relationships exist, and will these relationships develop? What rights do these individuals have? What power do you, as a researcher, have over those you study? To whom does data belong? What is the relationship you have with the people in your study? How will they engage with you? How will you use your findings (especially when your research is collaborative) to improve their human condition? We will dig more deeply into these kinds of questions as we go further into this book. We raise these issues now as an alert for what is to come.

As soon as you engage in collecting any data in a study, you are engaged in research—even if you just regard these efforts as "trying out," not as doing "real research." Legally, ethically, and morally, you are engaged in research when you begin to collect any data. You must investigate the permissions required and rules for access that are part of the context you study. For starters, we recommend that you investigate some of the many training modules available to researchers. There are legal requirements in all cases for human research. We would also encourage you to talk with the leaders in your contexts to see if there are rules or regulations for engaging in research.

Our Experience as Researchers

We are literacy teacher educators. Our experiences as researchers span decades and contexts. We have conducted small-scale and large-scale studies that include

- emergent literacy practices of young children;
- texts found in communities and classrooms;

- studies of performance assessment in literacy;
- literacy teaching (e.g., comprehension, drama, and fluency);
- literacy coaching;
- literacy instruction in developing countries;
- the role of communities in literacy development; and
- district-wide literacy reform efforts.

We have conducted studies that draw on and across various paradigms of research, including post-positivism, interpretivism, transformative, and pragmatic research (see Mertens's (2014) work).

In our hearts, though, we are practice-based researchers who study the teacher education programs in which we work, both for beginning teachers in our preservice teacher preparation program and for practicing teachers in our literacy specialist program. We are in a constant state of using research to grow our practices by employing both transformative principles and our radical imagination. We see this book as where we are today in our thinking and doing with practice-based research. We see this as a collective space and hope to engage you in thinking about ways in which we can grow our practices to better serve our young people and their communities in ways that foster social change.

Organization of This Book

We have organized this book around topics that are central to the role of researchers. In each chapter we will introduce concepts, suggest activities, and point toward additional resources. The book operates in two parts: Parts I and II. In the following section, we summarize the main points of these two parts and the chapters that are found within each.

Key Concepts in the Book

The first part of the book, "Part I: Background on Practice-Based Research," serves as a backdrop to practice-based research. This section is focused on inviting the reader (you) into the book and into a space of practice-based research with us. Part I is divided into four chapters.

In Chapter 1, "What Is Research, and What Counts as Research?," we introduce the basic frameworks and terminology that we use throughout the book (including clarifying the difference between research and inquiry and defining key terms and phrases). We use this chapter to situate our focus on practice-based research and the ways in which the radical imagination can support it.

In Chapter 2, "Why Should Classroom Teachers Engage in Research?," we begin with an examination of activity structures in classrooms to help readers think about places and spaces where they might begin to document their work with children in classrooms. These activity structures and the analysis of these activity structures can be thought of as "starting points" for thinking about practice-based research. We finish this chapter by encouraging our readers to think politically about what they do (e.g., why you do what you do) and how being in a state of reflexivity allows for the growth of radical imagination.

In Chapter 3, "The Roots of Practice-Based Research: Action Research," we begin with a general discussion of research methods. Then we move to consider one of the two emerging paradigms for research that are the focus for this book: practice-based research.

In Chapter 4, "The Roots of Practice-Based Research: Design-Development Research," we offer a description of a second approach to inform practice-based research: design-development research. Because there is no one way to engage in design–development research, we bring together some of the traditions that have informed this work and illustrate the potential of this approach for practice-based research.

In Chapter 5, "The Roots of Practice-Based Research: Transformative Research," we introduce transformational research as a third research tradition that informs our work in practice-based research. We demonstrate how transformational research assumes an activist stance toward research as a tool for social change and social justice. We explore youth participatory action research (YPAR) as a historical form of transformative work with children and youth and make connections between YPAR and practice-based research.

In Chapter 6, "Drawing Between and Across: Practice-Based Research," we formalize our use of the term *practice-based research* and commit to a set of features that define this work. We begin by positioning practice-based research in relation to other approaches used generally in educational research. We argue that practice-based research opens our profession up to a different set of tools, a different set of perspectives, a different set of questions, and a different set of potential contributions to both the improvement of literacy teaching and the professionalization of teaching as a practice.

In Part II, "Conducting Practice-Based Research," we focus on each of the elements of conducting practice-based research. We emphasize the cyclical, iterative, messy, and very complex nature of this type of research throughout the chapters in this section.

In Chapter 7, "Formulating Research Questions in Practice-Based Research," we discuss the process of generating research questions that can be studied using a practice-based approach. We discuss qualities of generative research questions and provide examples of research questions asked by teachers with whom we have worked.

In Chapter 8, "Situating Your Research Alongside the Research of Others," we illustrate the importance of connecting practice-based research with existing research. Through engaging in literature reviews, our readers will see how they are situating their work within an ongoing conversation about the topic(s) they have selected to study.

In Chapter 9, "Designing Your Study," we describe the cyclical steps to follow in planning for a study. The plan designed in this chapter will be inclusive of the generated questions addressed in Chapter 7. We will carefully consider the types of tools that teachers can use in conducting practice-based research.

In Chapter 10, "Interacting With Your Data," we take a comprehensive perspective on data, including how it is gathered, analyzed, and interpreted. We will encourage readers to be selective in the data collected for their study. We emphasize the cyclical nature of practice-based research.

In Chapter 11, "Sharing Your Work With Others," we emphasize the role of dissemination in supporting teachers as they engage in the research community and in their social obligation to sharing their research with other teachers and researchers. We provide various examples of how (and where) teachers can disseminate their research.

In our final chapter, Chapter 12, "The Practice-Based Researcher: Making the Road by Walking," we continue with the direction from the last chapter around the importance of sharing our work and return to the premise of the book, that becoming a transformative practice-based researcher using radical imagination is not an option for teachers, but a necessity and a responsibility. We encourage teachers to engage themselves and their colleagues in this type of research on an ongoing basis, as part of a larger community of practice. We situate our work for teachers as radical change agents in a more globalized movement for social change using the work of Hilary Janks (2009) to demonstrate that the everyday work of a classroom teacher (little "p" politics) is just as important (if not more so) than the seasonal work of politicians (big "P" politics).

Throughout the book you will encounter the work of people who have influenced our thinking, both in the writing of this book and over time. We invite you into the space with us to think with people you might expect to see cited in a book like this as well as more contemporary scholars whose thinking disrupts the traditional and puts us all in a space of reflection and reflexivity. And, in keeping with the academic work of these scholars, we have been intentional in the language we use in this book. Rather than talk about the people we find in K-12 classrooms (traditionally called *students*), we use the words children, youth, and/ or young people as a way of centering them in humanizing ways. Sometimes you may see us refer to the spaces in which learning takes place as *classrooms*; in other cases, we may call this space a *learning space*. Our point here is that words do matter; the language we use to talk about the young people with whom we work is indicative of what we believe about them, their capabilities, and who they are as people.

Centering on Classrooms and Teachers

We introduce several teachers to you throughout this book. Each of these teachers showed (and continues to show) us what it means to embody practice-based research. It is through peering into the practices of these teachers—looking into their classrooms and the ways in which they designed and are enacting practice-based research—that you might take on an imagined identity within an imagined community (Sailors, 2019). We have included artifacts from each of these classrooms and quotes from the teachers to help you imagine yourself as part of this community of practice-based researchers. You can find these teachers throughout the book—in some cases their stories are written directly into the text. In other cases, their stories can be found in the Meet the Teacher section of the eResources (www.routledge. com/9780367177607).

Making it Practical: Thinking and Doing Throughout the Book

Throughout this book, we will make the key concepts of each chapter practical by providing you with several ways to engage as you move through the book. First, each chapter begins with a "Points to Consider" insert. These inserts are intended to engage you in reflection from the onset of each chapter. We encourage you to journal or draw to reflect your way through the chapter considering the opening question. We will end each chapter by returning to these points in a section we call "Points to (Re)Consider." We will ask you to reflect on where you are in your thinking as a result (e.g., How has your thinking about X been affirmed or shifted as you have moved through this chapter?). We encourage you to journal through each chapter, fully prepared to reengage with these points.

Second, we will also present a "Pause and Reflect" section. These sections are designed to ask readers to stop and pragmatically apply the concepts of the chapter to their own work as practice-based researchers. For example, when we discuss engaging with our radical imagination, we will ask readers to think in terms of their own radical imagination—what aspects of their teaching draw upon their radical imagination and that of the youth with whom they work. It is our intention that these sections create a space where readers will reflect on how they can make the key concepts applicable to their daily lives as teachers.

Third, we offer "Engaging Children and Youth in Research" text boxes throughout each of the chapters. It is our hope that readers will see how they themselves are empowered by practice-based research and will be (even more) committed to engaging the children and youth with whom they work in research. And, not any research—research that draws from, capitalizes on, and builds the radical imagination of their children and youth. We will include at least one "Engaging" text box in each chapter.

Finally, we close off each chapter with sections we call "Reading Extensions," which suggest a set of readings that will extend your thinking beyond the boundaries of this book. The purpose of these "Reading Extensions" is to recognize that no one book can cover all the information you may want when engaging with a book. Likewise, we also believe there is much to still be considered when doing practice-based research that is beyond the scope of this book. We hope these "Reading Extensions" send the message that we are also (as we ask you to do) situating ourselves within various bodies of literature as part of a community of practice. You can find them on the eResource page (www.routledge.com/9780367177607).

We are excited you are here in this space with us. We hope you stay for a while and engage in the very type of practice we write about. And, we hope you reach out to us, as we would love to hear how you are using this book to transform not only your teaching but who you are and how you are in the world with children and youth, their communities, and other teachers.

References

Castoriadis, C. (1997). *World in fragments: Writings on politics, society, psychoanalysis, and the imagination* (D. A. Curtis, Trans. & Ed.). Stanford, CA: Stanford University Press.

Dewey, J. (1986). *A common faith: The collected works of John Dewey, 1882–1953* (J. A. Boydston, Ed.). Carbondale, IL: Southern Illinois University Press.

Haiven, M., & Khasnabish, A. (2017). *The radical imagination: Social movement research in the age of austerity*. London, UK: Zed Books.

Janks, H. (2009). *Literacy and power*. New York, NY: Routledge.

Ladson-Billings, G. (2006). From the achievement gap to the education debt: Understanding achievement in U.S. schools. *Educational Researcher, 35*(7), 3–12.

Mertens, D. M. (2014). *Research and evaluation in education and psychology* (4th ed.). New York, NY: Sage.

Sailors, M. (2019). Re-imagining teacher education. In D. E. Alvermann, N. J. Unrau, M. Sailors, & R. Ruddell (Eds.), *Theoretical models and processes of literacy* (7th ed., pp. 430–448). New York, NY: Routledge.

Vygotsky, L. S. (2004). Imagination and creativity in childhood. *Journal of Russian and East European Psychology, 42*(1), 7–97.

Background on Practice-Based Research

What is Research, and What Counts as Research?

Preview: Think of this chapter as background to the central focus for this book. We introduce some basic frameworks and terminology that will be used throughout the book. We also use this chapter to situate our focus on practice-based research.

Imagine this scenario:

Brenda: *"This old car is falling apart. We should start looking for a new one."*
Marcus: *"I think you're right. We should start by doing some research on affordable cars."*
Brenda: *"Right, I'll Google it."*

There are all kinds of ways in which we use the term *research*. Some uses seem quite casual, as in choosing a movie to see, while others are much more formal, such as the findings related to global warming. The similarities in the uses of this term are as important to explore as the differences. We will begin our examination of the term *research* in its informal uses and move to consider the kinds of research activity that are the focus in this book.

Points to Consider

Do you think this scenario describes an act of research? If so, why? If not, what would make it research?

Reflection and the Scientific Method

John Dewey, the preeminent educational philosopher of the 20th century, published a book in 1910 entitled *How We Think*. He centered his description of thinking on the reflective processes humans use as we engage with the social and physical world around us, developing the metaphor of "forks in the road" to describe the ways in which we engage with the challenges in daily life. These moments of decision-making can range from the relatively mundane (e.g.,

Should I drive to work today or take the bus?) to the more consequential (e.g., Who should I vote for in the next presidential election?). These moments of conscious decision-making trigger what Dewey called *reflective thinking*. Dewey talked about intentionally structuring classrooms so that children could learn to be reflective thinkers.

Dewey outlined the five steps in reflective thinking: First, one must identify and define the problem. Second, one must analyze the problem. Third, one must generate several possible (and viable) solutions. Fourth, one must evaluate options and select the best solution based on the evidence at hand or evidence gathered. Finally, one must test and implement the solution.

Over time, humans develop routines for how to deal with daily decisions, and the patterns of behavior become less a function of conscious reflective thinking and more a matter of "that's just the way I do this." We drive a car with only moments of active reflection. When new challenges are faced, however, our need to engage in reflective thinking surfaces. Such is the case when we are on the highway during rush-hour traffic and we realize that the exit we must take is coming up very quickly and we need to move over four lanes of traffic. We are now fully engaged in reflective thinking, although just moments before we were tapping our hand on the steering wheel to the beat of the music on our smartphone.

Dewey was a leader in the progressive educational movement (circa 1880–1940), and his model of individual thinking was closely aligned with the broader progressive movement sweeping all areas of society. The guiding principle of progressivism was that society can be improved through the systematic application of scientific thinking to the challenges we face—whether these challenges were part of the physical sciences (e.g., Is alternating current better than direct current? How can fertilizers be used to increase corn productivity?) or the social sciences (e.g., How do we improve worker efficiency in factories?). General Electric, founded by Thomas Edison in 1878, became a model for the progressive movement in industry, with its recurring themes around "progress is our most important product" and "imagination at work." Progressive education was rooted in the notion that experience should guide learning; many modern ideas of education draw from the progressive movement, including project-based learning, experiential learning, and collaborative and cooperative learning. And, according to Dewey (and others), imagination is at the heart of innovation.

Imagination and Scientific Methods

Early in the 20th century, Bowman (1936) cautioned researchers that it was their obligation to "implant pictures or conceptions in the reader's head like those which the investigator has in his" (p. 635) as part of their research report. He recognized that the research report was the space between what was in the writer/researcher's head (the "imagery") and what was in that of the reader. Some would argue that this is an archaic definition of *imagination* (as our "mind's eye"). Even so, imagination holds an ambiguous status (in many Western societies), thought of as a cognitive function in and of itself by some philosophers, while others believe it to be subservient to our intellect (or our minds).

Others believe in what is called a primary imagination (one not subject to our control) and a secondary imagination (which allows us to re-create new out of our "real" world). Even though this theory draws from the late 1700s, our society continues to believe, essentially, that "only artists can paint a beautiful picture because they were born with the ability"—that is, some people have control of their secondary imagination, but not all of us do. According to contemporary theories of imagination, this is an erroneous belief. In fact, more recent theories of imagination suggest that it is at the heart of all human endeavors, and tools that humans use are all a result of our shared imagination.

Recent theories indicate that our imagination is grounded in our experiences and is circular. That is, what we experience influences our imagination, while our imagination influences our experiences (Sailors, 2019). Studies from neurology indicate that humans combine elements of past experiences with "novel events" (those future events that we anticipate based on our imagination) as part of our adaptive process (Schacter et al., 2012). It is this adaptive process that has helped humans develop over time.

Scientific Theories, Knowledge, and Research

Of course, scientific thinking had a long history prior to progressivism, such as Newton's laws of physics and Ptolemy's representation of the motions of the moon, sun, and stars. These theories were all attempts to explain natural phenomena through the examination of evidence. There were also practical sides to this theoretical work (e.g., refinements in the calendar and in measuring time). In the classical tradition, the distinctions between philosophy and science were not as clearly marked as today. Aristotle was renowned for his observations of the sea, animals, and the universe and his investigation of causal relationships. The roots of Western science grew out of these philosophical traditions.

What distinguished the work of the progressive era from earlier work was the rapid expansion of scientific theories into practical applications in both the physical sciences (e.g., invention of the airplane, invention of the telephone) and the social sciences (e.g., constructs of intelligence in assessment), although some of this science was, with hindsight, for nefarious intent (e.g., eugenics). Research drove discovery. Research was the engine for dispelling some theories and introducing new ones. Research became the essential tool for the building of scientific knowledge. As its use expanded, the methods for doing research came under increasing scrutiny. What counts as research? Who gets to decide what counts? And, what ethical considerations should there be related to research? Professional communities of scientists focused in different disciplines began to create standards for what constitutes research and the ways in which research claims would be judged.

Universities, professional organizations, corporate entities with research and development divisions, and public institutions through their evaluation efforts began to formalize standards for research. Often, research methods grew inside of disciplines and then may have been shared or applied across others. Ethnography, for example, developed as a research methodology associated with studies of indigenous cultures from the field of anthropology. Many of the tools of ethnographic research have been adapted for use in educational research.

Pause and Reflect

- What role did classroom teachers play in establishing standards for research?

- What might be the impact of the lack of participation in research by teachers?

- What role should teachers play in the standardization of research?

Argument and Evidence as Key

Research is an inclusive term that involves different forms of activity. At the center of research, however, are studies that are bound by time, focus, and design. Through these studies, researchers gather evidence to inform understanding. In many cases, this information, often referred to as data, is collected in very small pieces. Data only becomes useful when it is analyzed in some fashion—data collected and then stored without being analyzed or discussed (such as all the data collected in many schools today) isn't really data, is it? Data is the record of the observations made and artifacts examined. Data becomes evidence as it is used to build an argument in support of a claim. Data is interpreted in the context of a question being posed and the theoretical frame being used to look at the data. Data often gets transformed in the processes of research. Data derived from student responses on a test is extrapolated and interpreted numerically. But data could also be a drawing that a child made, the talk in a discussion of a book, or a video of a coaching conference. Data varies by the area of inquiry. Data for a paleontologist might be a dinosaur's bone. Data for an epidemiologist may be the presence of a virus in a blood sample. What is common to all scientific research is the focus on empirical (i.e., verifiable through observation or experience) data. Data is always reported in scientific studies.

Collectively, studies often unfold in a series or sequence that forms a program of research. The understanding and explanations that emerge from research inform the scientific knowledge in a field. In some perfect world, this building of scientific knowledge would be conducted in a spirit of harmony. In fact, science and research are highly contested spaces. One scientist's representation of how words are recognized by a child in reading might stand in stark contrast to the representation of a different scientist. There may be three other scientists who have additional versions that contrast with those of the first two.

These kinds of contested spaces for scientific knowledge are critical to the building of scientific knowledge. The classical philosophers recognized the essential relationship between science and argument. It is in these spaces of argument that the work of scientific communities sorts out these claims and warrants and settles them within a community of peers.

Engaging in Research with Children and Youth

When we teach argument writing, we are teaching similar notions of research:

- What are the claims being made?
- What is the evidence for these claims?
- What processes were used to gather this evidence and to make these interpretations?

In legal deliberations, we see a similar kind of process. Claims are made based on evidence. Arguments are made that try to both make the case for the claims and discredit the arguments of the opposing side. The rules of evidence and the processes for deliberation are clearly defined. Ultimately, the judge (and/or jury) decides. The case ends, or it may be appealed to a higher court, and the case may become a defining case for legal precedent. Research claims are similarly argued, disputed, and adjudicated in the public space of professional journals. The internal review process of research reports (as they are submitted to a team of journal editors) is designed to ensure that (a) there is sufficient rigor in the methods used, (b) the warrants for the claims being made are firmly grounded in evidence, and (c) these claims contest or contribute to scientific knowledge. If these conditions are met (based on peer review), then the study is published and becomes part of what is known as a *literature* of a topic.

While no one study alone can provide the kind of scientific evidence on which important decisions about education can be made, all studies "fit" into a trajectory of a field's growth. The field of scientific knowledge (and what counts) can be inherently democratic if the process of public adjudication is followed carefully. For example, researchers often challenge the findings of the work of others. This happens in both the testing and retesting of hypotheses as well as in the challenging of the theoretical frames that researchers used to conduct their studies. For example, a widely published study by Hart and Risley (1995) described what the authors called a "vocabulary gap" between children who lived in what they called "wealthy" and "poor" neighborhoods. They claimed that it was the language deficiencies in children and families from "poor" communities that perpetuate the cycle of poverty. In one of the most cited aspects of their study, the authors claimed that (on average) a 3-year-old from a "poor" family demonstrated an active vocabulary of around 500 words, compared to the average 3-year-old from a "wealthy" family, who demonstrated a vocabulary of over 1,000 words. This difference, according to the research team, was linked to the differences in the vocabulary the children heard from their parents. This research led to a concept known as the "language gap," which in turn has led to public attention to the "problem" (Anders, Yaden, Da Silva Iddings, Katz, & Rogers, 2016) and decades of federal funding intended to "fix" children from "poor" communities.

More recently, this research has been critiqued for its methodological flaws, ethnocentric bias (that privileges middle- and upper-class linguistic and cultural practices), and failure to make explicit the theory that framed the analysis (Dudley-Marling & Lucas, 2009). Counterclaims illustrate how the original research "pathologized" people's language (Dudley-Marling & Lucas, 2009), treating their language as if it was abnormal. These were important counterclaims to make as part of checks and balances within educational research. Without counterclaims, research can be used to continue the oppression of people, their language, and their cultures.

These types of counterclaims are part of a necessary dialogue that takes place within scientific research. Researchers are trained to be critical of each other's work and rightfully so. As a result, questions arise from reading research reports: What theoretical frame was used for the study? How was data gathered (by whom and under what conditions)? How was it analyzed? How will the findings be applied? What are the politics behind the research? Finally, are there challenges to the study that should be taken up by individual researchers or the field? These are questions we should all ask of research, especially research that purports to frame people and their language and culture in ways that are harmful. Science is fundamentally democratic when it is working well.

Scientific Research is Scientific Research

There is a belief in universities (and in the public, in many cases) that what we do in the field of education is not really research. That is, social science research is "soft" and not as rigorous as so-called hard science research. This dichotomy is false and has been used (historically) to privilege some research over others. Our stance is that scientific research is a way of being in the world with inquiry and that what is typically called social science research is scientific in nature, as it seeks to answer questions and contribute to scientific knowledge. In fact, a graduate student that we work with recently confided that she was worried about doing research as her notions of research were grounded in numbers and statistical analysis and she was worried that she wasn't "up to it". Our point here is that there are many ways to engage in scientific research, and if we hold true to the spirit of systematic inquiry, we are "doing" research. We hope to continue to unpack these notions of what counts and what doesn't count as research as we continue this path in this book together.

Certainty in Science is Elusive

While some scientists believe there is certainty to the universe and other natural phenomena, we stand with those who believe that science (and scientific principles and concepts) are elusive, mainly because we (as humans) are limited by our tools. Our understanding of how language and literacy processes work and the principles we derive from our understandings will change as new tools and technologies are introduced. In fact, we can only describe our physical world through the apparatuses (tools) we have available to us (Barad, 2007). And, with the onset of new and improved apparatuses, the concepts we have (and hold) about the world around us can grow.

Take, for example, apparatuses used in quantum physics, the field that concerns the physical theories that explain the nuclear world, specifically nature at its smallest scales of energy levels of atoms and subatomic particles. One of the concepts studied by quantum physics is that of light and the age-old question: Is light a wave or a particle? As the apparatuses of science grew, so did our understanding of the answer to this question. While Newton's beliefs about the nature of light (that light was made of particles) held for many centuries, the earliest challenge to those notions were taken up by Thomas Young in 1801 in his (what is now famously called) double-slit experiment. It was through Young's work that the concept of light was forever changed. With his very simple device, which he called a "two-slit apparatus," he covered a window with a piece of paper that had only a single tiny hole in it, then held a single thin card in front of the beam of light that passed the hole, thus splitting the beam in two (hence the name "double-slit"). Young showed that the light that passed through the card interfered with the light from the other side of the card and created "fringes" (or waves) on the opposite wall. The question continued to be investigated in the 1920s by Einstein and Bohr, who disagreed about what would happen if Young's two-slit apparatus was modified (and subsequently, both invented revised apparatuses). Without belaboring their arguments, the concept of light as a particle or wave has shifted to "It depends," as many scientists today agree that the experiment (and the apparatus used) dictates what the researcher sees (Barad, 2007).

Similarly, the field of education is in a similar place—the way we "see" a concept (describe it, measure it, talk about it) is embedded inside our assumptions that we bring to the research, including our ontology (whose reality "counts" in research), our epistemology (how we know what we know), our axiology (the role of our values in our research), and our methodology (what method we choose to explore the questions we ask). These assumptions work in tandem and are the frames by which we engage in research. This is an important to think about because our awareness of our assumptions (as much as our assumptions themselves) influence the way we design and carry out studies.

While some think that the physical sciences offer more stable spaces for research, the reality is that there are deep divisions in research in the scientific world of research, too. Similarly, this is also true of educational research. Contested spaces are healthy for scientific inquiry as these become the "forks in the road" to guide future inquiry.

Research Does Not and Cannot Prove Anything

Statements like, "Research says . . ." and "Research proves . . ." without a mention of even a specific study that has been vetted through the public space of discussion should make you wary of anyone who is using these phrases. A scientist can gather evidence in support of a claim; that claim can never be "proven" to be true. The common causal claim that "smoking causes cancer" is based on decades of research. The evidence, accumulated over decades of research, is so strong that even courts have accepted this as a causal claim. But (to our knowledge) it is still not proven; in fact, the research is only correlational (smoking is associated, or correlated, with cancer). In contrast, a single study can disprove a theory or a claim. If someone makes a causal claim regarding a relationship of poverty (or ethnicity) to achievement, one case (or argument) can disprove that claim, as in the earlier example of the "language gap."

Skepticism is a Useful and Important Quality of Scientific Work

A dose of skepticism is a healthy part of scientific research as it is important that all claims put forward through research be doubted from the start. Science and scientists work at their best when they question and are skeptical of research, including that of their own and of others. Under a stance aligned with a healthy dose of skepticism, we are forced to examine the evidence and warrants (and theoretical frame, politics, and research methods) and not be swayed by the claims of findings. We design our own work and critique the work of others based on the understanding that evidence matters. Skepticism is different from cynicism. A cynic (one who believes people are motivated and act in self-interests) might say: "Research can be used to prove whatever you want." A skeptic (one who needs strong evidence in order to believe something) might say: "You need to convince me that I should believe the ways in which your data supports your claims."

The Danger in Dichotomies

Discussions of research and scientific methods are often bogged down by dichotomous thinking (this vs that). While these dichotomies are typically used in attempts to clarify discussions, they often lead to binary ways of thinking that limit the potential for research activity. In some worst-case scenarios, these dichotomies are used to discredit or disparage research, especially in the field of educational research. We believe that there is much to be gained in disrupting these binaries and opening possibilities. We raise three of these dichotomies here that are central to the focus for this book.

Evaluation Versus Research

Some studies are conducted with the purpose of gathering data to make decisions (e.g., Is this approach working in the ways that we planned? Are these materials being used, and if so, how?). When the decision-making process (formative or summative) is in the foreground, we tend to regard these types of studies as evaluative. That is, evaluation is usually a systematic determination of the merit and value of a program or practice. When the focus for a study is centered more on examining, extending, or challenging a theory, we tend to regard this as scientific research. In fact, the principles of design, evidence, and argument are highly aligned across these two activities. Both can contribute to knowledge. Subsequently, this is a false dichotomy.

Quantitative Versus Qualitative Research

This distinction is often associated with "objective versus subjective" notions of research. Both distinctions fall apart under scrutiny. Many people think of quantitative research as dealing only with numbers and qualitative research as dealing with everything that does not have numbers. However, the use of numbers in research (or not) does not divide approaches in any significant way. Observing and counting, to some degree, are common to almost all forms of research. Words and texts, as in the testing instruments used to derive scores, are common across almost all forms of social science research. More important distinctions and discussions are to be found in the epistemological stance (or, those assumptions about knowledge that reside below our beliefs and actions) taken in the research. What is the nature of the knowledge being explored? Is knowledge out there in the world waiting for us (as people) to discover it? Is our research attempting to uncover causal relationships among factors? Is our research attempting to understand context and represent interrelationships among processes? Is our research attempting to generalize from our studied sample directly to a larger group? The binary of quantitative versus qualitative does not address these and many other complexities of research methods. Our approach will be to name the research approaches that are the focus for this book and address the questions raised here without reference to this dichotomy. Subsequently, this, too, is a false dichotomy.

Experimental Versus Descriptive

Experimental studies test one or more variables to see "what works" and, oftentimes, under "what conditions"; they involve the manipulation of one variable (e.g., a method of teaching) and contrast that condition with a control condition in terms of results. There is a widely held belief within educational research that experimental studies are the most powerful form of research as if this type of research might lead to magical answers to complex questions. We question this position as it not only ignores the nature of what is being studied, it sets experimental versus descriptive as opposing possibilities for research. This may be the very place where the 'quant vs qual' dichotomy originated. However, we simply cannot accept this dichotomy as it simplifies the very nature of the complexity of research. In fact, the focus of this book, practice-based research, draws from the spirit of both of these fields of research. As in the previous two examples, this, too, is a false dichotomy.

Neutral Versus Engaged

The positionality of the researcher is important to consider in any research study. Positionality refers to the way in which researchers position themselves in reference to their data (e.g., is data there to "get" or is it "created" as a researcher moves through the study?) and the people in their study. For example, some researchers position themselves as "nonparticipant observers" and resist interacting with the people in their study; their belief is that they will influence their data too much if they interact. Other researchers position themselves as "participant observers" and deliberately interact with their participants. The way researchers position themselves determines when, how, and how much they will interact with the people in their study. At our very roots as classroom teachers, we have found it nearly impossible to collect data as nonparticipant observers, as it is very difficult to deny children assistance when they request it of us while we are collecting data. The image of research scientists, in either the physical or social sciences, as objective and distant is simply not true. Our passion for our topic is part of who we are as scientists. We do have a responsibility for making our positionality clear and accounting for the ways in which our position may be important to consider in examining the evidence and claims being made. We think you know what we are going to say about this as a dichotomy.

Theory Versus Practice

Kurt Lewin, a research scientist and educational philosopher of the early 20th century, is famous for this quote: "There is nothing as practical as good theory." We often use the corollary of this position in our work with teachers: There is nothing as theoretical as good practice. Theories are ways of explaining the world and the phenomena inside it; they are usually suppositions or systems of ideas. Theories and practice belong together as reflective, embodied ways of knowing the world. Theoretical frameworks are often named in research to situate the work within a frame (e.g., socio-constructivist theory, connectionism). We are cautious as well around the similar distinction between basic and applied research. The uses of research may be different, but the activities of research are more similar than different. There is no reason to believe that theories and practices live in opposition to each other.

> ### Pause and Reflect
>
> What are some other dichotomies related to research that you have heard or experienced? From where did they emanate? Why should we be cautious of them?

Trustworthiness

Can you trust what you read that claims research as its base? We would like to respond to this with a resounding "yes," but caution is advised. Suffice it to say that there is tremendous variability in the quality of journals. Journals that report research are arrayed on a continuum, from journals that are highly rigorous and competitive to those that are less selective, with lower standards, and with very high acceptance rates. All of these journals may apply peer-review processes, but the standards are different. It is also worth noting that there are many professional journals that publish articles that address important topics but do not report actual research. These journals may be valuable in many ways, but the articles should not be interpreted as reports of research. Other concerns regarding trustworthiness are important to mention as well. Finelli (2009) reported the results of a survey study in which 14% of scientists claimed to know a scientist who fabricated entire data sets, and 72% said they knew a scientist who had indulged in other questionable research practices, such as dropping selected data points to sharpen study results. A study reported in the journal *Nature* (Baker, 2016) found that "more than 70% of researchers have tried and failed to reproduce another scientist's experiments, and more than half have failed to reproduce their own experiments" (p. 452). Is it any wonder that the public has such a distrust of research?

The term *publication bias* refers to the fact that most research journals tend to accept and publish studies that report significant findings (versus studies that show no significant findings or no impact). So, the one study that is submitted to a journal with significant results (e.g., exploring the relationship between early literacy and college entry) will be published. The five studies that have examined this relationship and found no relationship will not be published. The impression conveyed in research journals is often that everything seems to work out in a positive direction, when the reality may be quite different. And, how much more would we know in our field if studies that had no direct impact were published?

Again, we reiterate that we are not cynical about research but rather take on a healthy skepticism in accepting the claims made by researchers in publications. We are prepared to ask hard questions of all research reports.

Paradigms and Mistakes

Thomas Kuhn (1962/1996), in his book *The Structure of Scientific Revolutions*, challenged the view of science and research as the gradual accumulation of knowledge informed by research over time (what he called "development by accumulation"). Instead, he offered a view of science as periods of gradual growth that are punctuated by revolutionary moments. One of the prime examples he used is the shift from the Ptolemaic representation of planetary movements to the Copernican system. He framed these moments of punctuated growth as paradigm shifts. Simply said, paradigms are concepts or thought patterns of the world. In the field of education, paradigms include theories, research methods, and standards for what "counts" within the field. With a change in basic assumptions, scientists recognized how our previous ways of viewing were shaped by a set of assumptions that were flawed—and with a new perspective, the path of planetary science was changed. As paradigms shifted, so too did our understanding of the world.

We see the influences of these paradigm shifts in educational research as well. In the mid-20th century, researchers in reading were consumed with questions around certain subjects: What is the "best time" for beginning reading instruction? What measures can we use to determine readiness for reading? How can we accelerate the readiness process and get students (their word, not ours) reading earlier? What happens to students (same) who enter first grade and cannot read? Then, a group of researchers stepped in with a series of studies that were focused on questions such as, What sense can we make of the reading and writing of children from birth moving forward? This movement led to the field of emergent literacy, and it was a punctuated moment that in just a few years changed the nature of the questions we were asking about early literacy. This was a change in basic assumptions. The breakthrough to this new paradigm came not just as the result of conceptual work but in a shift to using new approaches to research. The scribbling marks of young children became marks to be interpreted. Engaging in conversations with young children around their work—engaging them and asking them to consider, What did you write?—was essential to this breakthrough.

Research as Power

If knowledge is power, then whoever has control of research has a lot of control over power. It is occupational and there are rewards for it—successful researchers reap benefits (e.g., patents, promotions, consultancies, support for future work). And, while we tend to think about research as intellectual, it is moral and political work as well. Who gets to do research is shaped by who has access to funding. What research is supported is often shaped by priorities set by funding agencies, who are often advised by successful researchers. You see the cycle.

The clearest evidence for the political side of research is found in education research over the past three decades. Experimental research has been set as the gold standard for research support, and this research receives the bulk of federal funding. This is a purely political decision, not a decision based on science or evidence of research that has contributed to practice.

Likewise, classroom teachers have historically (and politically) not been perceived as researchers—not in the "true" sense of the word. Over time, there has been a growing movement to recognize and validate the systematic inquiry and insight that teachers bring to the research table. This is the space in which this book resides. Our stance is that practice-based research engages and convokes the radical imagination of classroom teachers (as well as our own) and reduces the schism often found between theory and the problem to be solved in practice. Tapping into (and developing and growing) the radical imagination of teachers allows for the exploration of possibilities for classrooms that are different from those of today, both for the present (today) and for the future. We'll talk more about the radical imagination in subsequent chapters.

Pause and Reflect

What other "truths" about literacy have been shifted or debunked because of shifting/growing paradigms?

Summary

We are optimistic for the future of educational research but not oblivious to the challenges that face us. Scientific research, like reflective thinking, begins with a problem or a challenge. We engage within that space to understand or make change. We gather data and analyze the data toward an understanding. We make

Points to (Re)Consider

Return to the opening scenario. Were your initial thoughts affirmed throughout this chapter? Challenged? Developed? In what ways?

claims from this data. We open our work to the critical inspection of others. This is the essence of scientific research. It sounds a little easier on paper than in reality; that is the challenge we must rise to meet.

The good news is that the rest of the book is focused on the positive side of research and the potential for practice-based research in the future. We can only trust that the politics of research, which have become so narrowed, will become more expansive and democratic based on the kind of research advanced in this book and its effects on teaching and schools.

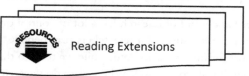

Reading Extensions

References

Anders, P. L., Yaden, D. B., Da Silva Iddings, A. C., Katz, L., & Rogers, T. (2016). Editorial: More words for the poor? Problematizing the "language gap." *Journal of Literacy Research, 48,* 131–133.

Baker, M. (2016). Is there a reproducibility crisis? *Nature, 533*(7604), 452–454.

Barad, K. M. (2007). *Meeting the universe halfway: Quantum physics and the entanglement of matter and meaning.* Durham, NC: Duke University Press.

Bowman, C. C. (1936). Imagination in social science. *American Sociological Review, 1,* 632–640.

Dewey, J. (1910). *How we think.* Boston, MA: D. C. Heath.

Dudley-Marling, C., & Lucas, K. (2009). Pathologizing the language and culture of poor children. *Language Arts, 86,* 362–370.

Finelli, D. (2009). How many scientists fabricate and falsify research? A systematic review and meta-analysis of survey data. *PLoS ONE, 4*(5), e5738. doi:10.1371/journal.pone.0005738

Hart, B., & Risley, T. R. (1995). *Meaningful differences in the everyday experiences of young American children.* Baltimore, MD: Brookes.

Kuhn, T. S. (1996). *The structure of scientific revolutions* (3rd ed.). Chicago, IL: University of Chicago Press. (Original work published 1962)

Sailors, M. (2019). Re-imagining teacher education. In D. E. Alvermann, N. J. Unrau, M. Sailors, & R. Ruddell (Eds.), *Theoretical models and processes of literacy* (7th ed., pp. 430–448). New York, NY: Routledge.

Schacter, D. L., Addis, D. R., Hassibis, D., Martin, V. C., Spreng, R. N., & Szpunar, K. (2012). The future of memory: Remembering, imagining, and the brain. *Neuron Review, 76,* 677–694.

2 Why Should Classroom Teachers Engage in Research?

Preview: We will focus the bulk of this chapter on the inspection of your work as a teacher and the ways you might already be engaged in research as you explore and extend your teaching practice.

Try saying this aloud: "I am a researcher." For some of you, this will roll right off the tip of your tongue. For others, you may pause (perhaps you have still not even tried to say it). Still others may have said it, but with some trepidation. There are many reasons for the various responses you might have to our invitation. You may not (yet) believe it to be true. You may be saying, "Wait, I'm only starting Chapter 2. Give me some time." Fair enough. We totally understand and we have been there ourselves. Building a researcher identity takes time, experience, commitment, and a community to support you.

> ### Points to Consider
>
> What is your identity as a researcher? Are there aspects of research that you are comfortable with? Others that you want to grow toward?

Developing our identities as researchers is an ongoing process. We are all in a state of "becoming" as researchers as we learned through Theresa Nguyen's practice-based research study. At first, Theresa believed that research belonged to "scientists" rather than classroom teachers. But, as her study progressed, she soon began to believe that all teachers should see themselves as practice-based researchers and should engage in practice-based research.

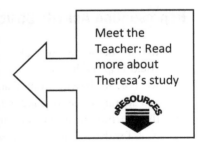

Meet the Teacher: Read more about Theresa's study

Literacy Teaching

The context for our work, as practice-based researchers, is in our classrooms. We could have approached the writing of this chapter from a very academic stance where we would have defined teaching, related the history of teaching, described approaches to teaching, and summarized findings from research on teaching. We have chosen a different path for reasons that are tied directly to our goal of promoting practice-based research. Teaching is a combination of what teachers do and their understanding of why they do what they do. More specifically, teaching is *what* you do, *why* you do what you do, and *who* you do this with in the context of a classroom space. While this may sound superficial and non-critical, you will see that the careful examination of these processes can lead to a very deep understanding of teaching practices. We focus our examples on literacy, but the same processes could be applied across all disciplines and contexts.

We have found it helpful to ask teachers with whom we work to describe a typical day to help us understand the framing of their practice and how they think (and talk) about their teaching. We ask them to sketch out what they do and, more important, what their young people are doing as they move through the day. We make note of the words and labels teachers use to describe their work. Sometimes, teachers' terminology may reflect the localized activities in their classrooms (e.g., "We start each day with a poem and end the day with a class meeting"). In other cases, teachers may talk about the commercial programs afforded to them in their classrooms (e.g., "We use iStation to practice phonics, and our basal reader drives our whole-group instruction"). In still other cases, teachers may use terms that represent methodologies or routines, including (but not limited to) read alouds, mini-lessons, writing workshop, and guided reading. At the surface level, this might look like a class schedule that uses terms that the teacher and the students share. There is a deeper level of analysis, though, that can reveal the pedagogical structures that undergird the activities because the way they frame their practice is quite complex.

When we examine teachers' descriptions of their classrooms, we come to see them in what we will term *activity structures*. These activity structures are bounded by time, goals, participation structures, products and artifacts, spaces, movement, and expectations for success. These are routines in the sense that they are predictable, as they repeat themselves each day. The content may vary (e.g., the book that is read, the strategy that is in focus, the artifacts that are produced), but the structure for the activities remains consistent. Teachers (with their students) have internalized these structures and cooperate and collaborate in enacting them successfully in the classroom.

Representing Activity Structures

In some of the earliest work on teaching, researchers thought in terms of how activity structures could help teachers think about the teaching and learning in their classrooms. In this section, we borrow heavily from that work as a starting place for thinking about the structures in your classroom, your goals for these activity structures, and how you are thinking about changes you would like to make in your teaching. We believe this path into examining your own practices might help you begin to think about and identify those parts of your practice

Pause and Reflect

- What are some of your activity structures?
- What are the goals of those activity structures?
- What do you value about those activity structures?

for your practice-based research. If this feels as if we are starting from a place of reflection, we are. But, we will move quickly into reflexivity as we progress through this book. We will begin with a consideration of two kinds of components—*critical* and *optional*—and then will move to consider *variations* on components.

Critical Components

The first components of an activity structure are known as *critical components*. They are the most important elements of an activity as their presence (on a daily basis) allows for the activity to fulfill its goals. The critical components of an activity structure refer to the things teachers intend to be present in their teaching. For example, in a read aloud activity structure, a critical component might be a "quality literature selection" as the type of text a teacher brings to the read aloud may be one of the most important decisions to make in planning for the activity. During literature circles, a critical component might be the way in which youth participate in conversations about their text—they can engage either with preselected (usually by the teacher) responses (e.g., "What was the most important event that happened in the chapter?") or through youth-generated responses (e.g., "OMG! Can you believe the character did that? What in the world was he thinking?"). Without either of these components, neither activity would yield its intended goals.

The process of identifying and describing the components of the activity structures sounds straightforward, but it can become quite complex and can serve as a window into a teacher's philosophy. And, as such, we would expect that different teachers would identify different critical components for their various activities. When we refer to the critical components of an activity structure, we are not attempting to judge what a teacher is doing in a writer's workshop according to some external standard but rather are digging into each teacher's intentions for enacting an activity structure. One teacher's writer's workshop might be open to children choosing the topic and the genre for their work. A different teacher's writing workshop may restrict children to a genre but leave freedom around the topic. In considering the critical components in a classroom, we do not judge one as right or one as wrong, one as better or one as worse. We regard them as different but equally important.

Optional Components

Invariably, in the construction of activity structures, we come to components that are only sometimes there. For example, a teacher described an optional component of her read aloud: "In my read alouds, I really like to get the kids physically involved in the book experience. We often use drama to do this. It's doesn't happen all the time, but I think it's important in building comprehension." The teacher was talking about drama as an optional component to her activity structure for a read aloud. The label is not intended to suggest "not important" but just not present every time. This optional component is used selectively based on circumstances. In the previous example, the teacher may see some read aloud selections as more suitable for drama than others. And, when drama is not present, she is (more than likely) engaging her young people in another optional component, such as an artistic response to the read aloud.

In another classroom, a teacher described "book selection" as a critical feature of her read aloud practice. She reported, "I try to choose books that are high in literary quality, touch on something important, and are current in my children's lives. I invite them to examine situations from multiple perspectives. That's when it is really good." But this is not always the case. "Sometimes," she said, "I may choose a book that doesn't meet all of these qualities, but the minimum is that I choose books that have high literary quality." This is common. Even though the goal of the read aloud activity structure is to engage in notions of social justice, sometimes we want to engage young people in books that have beautiful art in them, as books commonly serve as children's first entry into the world of art. In this example, the teacher may see some read aloud selections as more suitable for conversations about social issues than others. And, when conversations about social issues are not present, she is (more than likely) engaging her young people in another optional component, such as conversations about the peritextual features of books (Martinez, Stier, & Falcon, 2016).

Variations in Components

There is a third component to activity structures that considers the variations that may occur within an activity structure. This is a particularly important component to consider when looking at your own classroom. Variations can range from a typical variation (standard types of shifts that are made within an activity structure) to those variations that happen under ideal circumstances, or in the words of one teacher, "on a very good day." Likewise, on "not so very good" days, these variations appear to teachers to be "not acceptable." For example, in a conversation with the same teacher who is mapping out the critical features of her read aloud in the classroom, she told us the following:

> On a typical day, we engage in a read aloud for 30 minutes. That is my standard. On a great day, we might extend this to 40 minutes. Some days it just works out to be just 20 minutes; that is obviously a variation that is not my ideal, but that sometimes happens. There are days where we do not get to the read aloud at all; those are very rare. That's obviously not okay, and I work hard to make sure this does not happen very often.

The critical component in this teacher's classroom is time, and that is the component that varies. Within variability, there is an internal standard for each component that is the minimum set by the teacher.

Documenting Activity Structures

Teachers enact activity structures on a regular basis; we believe that writing them down and documenting those structures can be an important starting place for thinking about a practice-based research study. To that end, we are going to ask you to document your activity structures, organizing them following the components and features we described earlier (critical components, optional components, and variations in components). In documenting them, we can "hold the features still" to examine them and interrogate them. This is the first step in practice-based research. The process of identifying and describing makes the invisible visible. Making these activity structures visible is also a first-level analytical step toward practice-based research.

Here, we introduce you to one way a teacher might documented a set of activity structures in her classroom. We offer this example in the hope that it will assist you in your identification and description of the activity structures that guide your work. Figure 2.1 illustrates what this teacher identified as the critical components of her read aloud. Figure 2.2 illustrates what that same teacher identified as the optional components of her read aloud.

You can see from the critical and optional components that this teacher has carefully thought about her read aloud activity structure. While it might take several conversations with others around her in order for her to isolate and describe those features you see in the figures, most teachers find this helpful as it allows them to see inside several of the components where they might want to begin to focus their practice-based research project.

While deconstructing activities into components can yield insights, we must exercise caution in our thinking about these components as independent elements. The components of

	On a good day...	**In my ideal classroom (in addition to the "on a good day") ...**
My book selection	I use high quality, children's literature. I relate my selections to the interests of my children. My books are connected thematically (or in other ways) each week. The book will likely evoke a strong aesthetic response from my children. The text should enhance and/or challenge their prior knowledge, beliefs, and values.	The books I chose are likely to become an anchor text for work that is done throughout the year in writing and work in other areas. The book is likely to spark children's imagination and curiosity toward inquiry projects and multi-model response activities both in school and out of school.
I read with expression	I read with a lot of expression (appropriate volume and articulation). I let the author's words carry the momentum of the experience.	I incorporate drama (e.g., with character voices, props, movement) as I read the book. I encourage my children to participate as appropriate.
I create spaces where my children can talk about the book	I give my children many opportunities (at appropriate times) to talk using pair share, think-alouds, and child-initiated responses. I try to keep the talk to a minimum so it does not detract from the rhythm of the text.	I am sensitive to the need for my children to talk during the read aloud—I watch their faces and body language. As a result, there is a high level of child-initiated responses.
The role of my talk in the read aloud	I am explicit about why I chose the book for the read aloud. I start by activating my children's prior knowledge and continue to do so throughout. I model my thinking during the read aloud and invites my children to do the same. My talk is only at important junctures in the text and does not detract from the rhythm of the text being read. If my children have copies of the text (e.g., in a 'read along' setting) then I incorporate this access into the discussion (e.g., let us look at what the author says here)	I focus on comprehension strategies (e.g., imagery) as part of my think aloud process. I explicitly explain the strategy before reading. My attention to the strategy does not become foregrounded nor does it detract from the text.

FIGURE 2.1 Critical Components of a Read Aloud

	On a good day...	In my ideal classroom (in addition to the "on a good day") ...
The way I use images	I actively model the use of images in the text to construct meaning. I use the images to evoke responses and nuances of the meaning of the text. This includes images in fictional and informational texts.	Through modeling and interactions with my children, I explicitly examine the ways in which the illustrator (both stylistically and in the composition of the illustration) extends the author's words.
Supporting vocabulary development	I pay attention to developing word meanings as part of the read aloud experience. I am selective in what words I focus on so as not to overwhelm the reading.	During reading, the children and I gather words; we use them later for our word study and prominently display them around our classroom.
Leaving a trail of text behind...	My children and I create texts because of our read aloud. These texts are organized and displayed in our classroom in ways that value their active co-construction of the texts.	My children use the texts we create in their writing.
Frequency and time	I engage in a read aloud three or four days per week for approximately 20 minutes each.	I engage in a read aloud every day for 25 minutes.
Management of time and space	My children are comfortable; they all can see / hear the read aloud. I remind them of our classroom expectations for participation.	My children can see the text and me AND each other as a way of facilitating discussion.

FIGURE 2.1 (Continued)

	On a good day...	In my ideal classroom (in addition to the "on a good day") ...
I make connections to the curriculum	I make an explicit attempt to relate the read aloud experience to targeted curriculum outcomes for reading and the language arts.	I make an explicit attempt to relate the read aloud experience to targeted curriculum outcomes for other content areas (e.g., math, science, social studies).
I point out the craft of the author	I explicitly discuss the craft of the author and illustrator so my children see the connection to writing.	I use the read aloud as a basis for writing across the genres.
Readers' theater	I incorporate readers' theater (and other forms of dramatic activity) into the read aloud.	I incorporate readers' theater and other forms of dramatic activity into response activities that follow our read alouds.
Inquiry	I use the context of the text and children's 'wonderings' as the basis for research that is brought back into the discussion of the read aloud.	I engage in full inquiry projects because of the read aloud (e.g., read aloud serves as a portal into an inquiry project).
Complementary texts	I display a collection of complementary texts that relate thematically to the read aloud in an attractive manner. I provide access to these other texts for the children during their independent reading time.	I make the complementary texts available for children to check out and take home to share with their families. I create spaces where they can share the response of their family to the texts in my classroom the following day(s).

FIGURE 2.2 Optional Components of a Read Aloud

an activity structure are highly interactive and cannot and should not be isolated from the whole. A good example of this error can be seen in programs to support the development of fluency. We can decompose the construct of fluency in literacy to a componential structure of accuracy, rate, and expression. While this analytical perspective can offer us a useful lens for observing and understanding fluency, we cannot isolate our work with children on fluency with a focus on one of the components to the exclusion of the others. The activity structure for a read aloud combines many components, but we cannot separate work on book selection, for example, without a simultaneous consideration of all the components working in unison for the children.

Pause and Reflect

- Pick an activity structure in your classroom and identify and describe the critical and optional components.
- Where are your variations?
- How does making your practice visible inform your practices?

The Individual Teacher and the Community of Practice

Thus far, we have described the activity structures that individual teachers enact. It is also possible to think about these activity structures within a community of practice. This notion of a community of practice, which we will expand on in future chapters, encourages us to think about practice-based research as something that can be collaborative in nature. Teachers may come together to examine individual activity structures that are shared in name (e.g., workshop) but through the exploration of the activity structure find important differences. These differences can become entry points for change as we create new activity structures out of the variations that exist among our community.

While the outcomes associated with inspecting our own activity structures are almost always positive, there is a danger that this kind of work toward a shared version of an activity structure in a community of practice can become oppressive rather than expansive. The written representation of an activity structure could become an observational checklist where standardization becomes the goal. There becomes a right way and a wrong way. This caution should not deter our work with activity systems or our work together but rather serve to remind us that we are at our best when we do less judging of and more learning with each other.

Activity Structures in Motion

Let us now examine your activity structures as they unfold in your practice. Despite all our careful planning and intentionality, teaching almost never unfolds as we expect. We, as teachers, are in a constant mode of making changes while we are teaching as we meet with the unexpected. Forks in the road appear that require we decide on a path to take. What do we do when we are reading *Separate Is Never Equal: Sylvia Mendez and Her Family's Fight for Desegregation* (Tonatiuh, 2014) and a child calls out, "They should just all go back to

Mexico!"While it may not surprise you, you hadn't planned on this at all. What do you do? It is a fork in the road, rich with possibilities for discussions with the young people in your classroom.

Donald Schön (1983, 1987) extended Dewey's conception of reflection to the work of professionals. He studied professionals from across areas (e.g., architects), including teachers. What he found was that reflection played a central role in what people considered to be a successful practitioner. The essence of professional life is making important decisions in the moment within complex spaces. And, those spaces are almost always changing. Schön described two types of reflection: reflection in action and reflection on action.

Reflection in action refers to the shifts we make in the moment as we respond to the unexpected. Some adjustments may be very subtle, while some can involve major shifts in the flow of the activity. Our good friend Gerry Duffy refers to this work of teachers as being "thoughtfully adaptive" (Duffy et al., 2008). He regards these moves as the essence of powerful practice. Consider the complexity of this kind of teaching. First, the teacher must recognize that something unexpected (and important) has happened. Second, the teacher must consider, in just seconds, the range of options of response and the merits of each in this context. Third, the teacher must engage with the option chosen and then adjust the entire activity structure moving forward. Duffy regards these as windows into a teacher's practice. As teachers, we recognize that these moments are not rare at all. In many ways, these are the life of teaching.

Schön's second type of reflection, *reflection on action*, refers to the kind of thinking that teachers do as they look back on a teaching experience. As teachers, we recognize these as the "should've" and "could've" types of second-guessing that we do. Some of this reflection on action is focused on planning for components of future activity structures (e.g., book choices for the next read aloud). Other reflections on action center on the in-practice reflection moves we made (e.g., taking time to stop and review a mini-lesson that might not have been taken up by our youth). There is another kind of reflection on action that we describe as *refraction*. This is where we take what we learned from a teaching experience and think forward to the next day or into adjustments to that activity structure itself. For some teachers, this might be a long-term refraction cycle (e.g., "Next year, I will . . ."), while for other teachers this refraction cycle might be almost immediate (e.g., "Well, that didn't work well at all in my first-period class. I think I will change up some things for second period"). Both are important to thinking about our practice as teachers and engaging in practice-based research.

As you engage in reflection, we hope you see it as an exercise to help you become aware of (and act upon) the thinking that you do during times of uncertainty, uniqueness, and instability in your classroom (reflection in action). It is also intended to help you become aware of (and act upon) the thinking that you do as you engage in planning for subsequent activity structures (reflection on action). Most often, it is helpful to reflect with a colleague, where possible.

Pause and Reflect

- Return to your Activity Configuration. What would your reflection in action look like? What would your reflection on action look like?

What About Curriculum?

We have been intentional in not using the term *curriculum* to describe the work of representing practices. John Dewey (1964) defined curriculum "as a continuous reconstruction, moving from the learner's present experience out into that represented by the organized bodies of truth that we call studies" (p. 344). A curriculum is typically described in terms of courses and lessons taught, including both the intended curriculum (curriculum materials or district or state documents) and the hidden curriculum (those messages we send to young people about whose voices count and whose do not). We view activity structures as the bridge between the experiences of the child and the organized learning goals represented in a curriculum. In the end, a teacher must be able to draw the lines that connect the activity structures to these goals.

What Is the Basis for Your Activity Structures?

Now that you have started to think about your activity structures and the ways in which you can reflect on them, there remains one more aspect to consider about practice-based research. We often engage ourselves and the teachers with whom we work in conversations about the roots of the activity structures themselves. Read the following questions we pose, thinking in terms of at least one (or more) of your activity structures.

- Where do these activity structures come from? Are they your own invention? From a commercial program? From a colleague? When did these activity structures become part of your practice? How did they enter? How have they changed?

- What learning and growth is promoted by participation in these activity structures? What evidence do you have that these activity structures yield what you intend? Have you dug into how your students think about these activity structures and why you do what you do?

- How do all the different activity structures in your teaching link together? Are they all necessary? Do you worry about how these are aligned with school, district, and state expectations and standards? What is the argument you make in defense of what you do in an activity structure if you are questioned or challenged?

In addressing these kinds of questions, you are beginning to reveal your practices and your teacher identity as a practice-based researcher. Are you convinced yet?

Paradigms and Double-Loop Learning

Humans are creatures of habit, and this often means reducing the amount of reflection we do in the work with the mundane so we can focus on the more important decisions or just relax, go with the flow, and not stir up the water. We think within the paradigms within which we live. And, until we begin to question the paradigms, there is no need to engage in critical questions about how our teaching maintains the status quo. Donald Schön apprenticed with Chris Argyris. Together they wrote about another kind of reflection that they referred to as *double-loop learning.* This type of learning pertains to learning to change underlying values and assumptions (Argyris & Schön, 1974).

In single-loop reflection, we engage with the unexpected within a range of responses that we have used in the past. For example, the principal of our elementary school is coming down hard on noise in the halls because of what he refers to as "sloppy lines." We understand what he wants. We tighten the ship. We try what we know to do to get our kids to walk in a straight (and quiet) line. We ask them to put bubbles in their mouths. We ask them to put their hands behind their backs and walk on the squares. When that does not work, we appoint the "problem kids" as the line leaders. When that does not work, we go back to the room and start all over. We make two lines—one for boys and one for girls. We have class meetings and we make anchor charts to describe all the qualities of a good line and good movement in the halls. We reward. We deny recess. We make kids write a hundred times: "I will not talk in line in the halls" (wait, that's too far even for us).

But when do we ask the questions, Why are we lining up? Why do we have to walk single file in the halls? What is lining up with bubbles in your mouth and hands behind your back really preparing students for? Suddenly, these practices that we have accepted and embodied begin to look prisonlike. That is not what school is about—or is it?

These are the types of questions that double-loop learning gets at; it

Pause and Reflect

Go back to the activity structures that are at the core of your teaching practices. On what assumptions are these based? How are these assumptions limiting the possibilities of teaching? How can these assumptions be challenged in ways that better serve our students?

pushes back against the conditions and assumptions that surround single-loop reflection. This type of reflection asks us to examine the conditions we assume are fixed and the powers that hold these conditions in place. The lining-up example is just the start. There are many more. And, they are hidden in places where we least expect to find them.

Radical Imagination: Reflexive Thinking and "What-If's"

What if? What if we took away all the labels we have placed on kids: "My tier-three kids," "my GT kids," "my ESL kids"? What if we removed all the limits on teachers that deny their professionalism: "Everyone must attend this PD" or "We are all going to do writing workshop"? What if we turned the curriculum over to the children and youth we teach: "What challenges in our community can we solve? How can we use math or language arts to address those challenges?" What if we looked at all our activity structures and said: "What if I had total freedom to teach my young people to be literate in the critical sense of the word?"

Schools, for a variety of social, political, and historical reasons, tend to do a better job of squashing curiosity than engaging it and teaching it. There are few spaces in schools today for teachers and young people to exercise their imagination. But, isn't that what education is supposed to do? To grow and nurture imagination? That said, we believe many teachers (other than primary teachers) do not engage the imagination of young people because they themselves may not see the value of it with older children and youth. For many, discussions about imagination are relegated to early childhood education, and beyond that (in youth and adulthood), imagination seems to ignored. What if developing and invoking the imagination of all young people (very young children, children, and youth) were at the center of education?

To ask "what if" questions that push on double-loop learning, we must engage and convoke our radical imagination (Castoriadis, 1997). The concept of *radical* draws from the Latin *radix*, or "root" and helps us understand that social, political, economic, and cultural challenges and issues are outcomes of societally rooted tensions, contradictions, power imbalances, and forms of exploitation in our society (Haiven & Khasnabish, 2017). To engage our radical imagination is to ask "what if" questions that challenge deeply rooted practices that have been passed down through the generations of our profession. At the basic level, our radical imagination allows us to envision our social institutions (and a world) not as they are but as how they might be. At a deeper level, our radical imagination can not only bring into existence that which is new and novel within our world of experience (and that of others); it can also create new experiences not represented elsewhere (Haiven & Khasnabish, 2017).

Engaging in Research with Children and Youth

As we are teaching young people to explore their natural world and act as risk-takers and problem solvers, we teach them to ask questions, such as:

- What if we were to combine these two (substances in science, for example)? What might the outcome be?

- What if we were to extend this last note a bit longer (when revising a piece of music we are working on)? What might the outcome be?

- What if we were to revise the end of the story so that the dog does not die (when we are rewriting famous novels)? What might the outcome be?

One argument that we have made elsewhere is that while reflective thinking (single-loop reflection) is an important part of teaching, it is simply not enough to expose contradictions and injustices (Sailors, 2019). What is required is known as *reflexivity* or critical reflexive practice. Reflexivity allows us to recognize, highlight, and address tacit assumptions and to decodify structures of oppressive power and authority in our personal lives and in our daily practices as teachers. It is through reflexivity that we realize that our foundations were handed down to us by our social institutions. Reflexivity is only possible through the engagement of our radical imagination, which is convoked through "what if" questions that we ask ourselves and others.

One teacher, Ellen Webber, thinks in terms of growing her practice as it relates to one or more of the activity structures in her classroom. In her practice-based research, she wanted more dialogue among her young people during the read aloud. She could have given them more opportunities to "turn and talk" to each other. But, because she was convoking her radical imagination, she asked herself a "what if" question: "What if I didn't tell them when to talk? What if I just let them talk when they felt the need to say something?" And, "What if I didn't have them raise their hands and wait for me to call on them? What if they simply talked to each other the way we do outside of school?" These are the kinds of questions that placed Ellen in a place of questioning the very foundations of her teaching—and put her in a place of exploring where her practices (e.g., "Raise your hand and wait until I call on you to speak") come from.

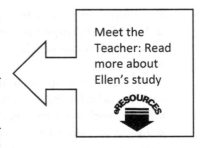

Meet the Teacher: Read more about Ellen's study

eRESOURCES

Of course, some people would respond by saying, "If I did those kinds of things in my classroom, I'd be fired."
We believe that this is an untested assumption, and we will explore these assumptions in other sections of the book. But for now, we will take a more strategic approach.

Transformative Practice-Based Research: A Journey

Why must teachers engage in research? Research is not a choice. It is a moral obligation for all professionals. We bear a responsibility to learn individually and collectively. We also have a social and moral obligation to our young people to serve them in the best ways we can (re) imagine. That's what transformative, practice-based research is all about. Paulo Freire (1971) describes it best in this statement:

> The more radical the person is, the more fully he or she enters reality so that, knowing it better, he or she can transform it. This individual is not afraid to confront, to listen, to see the world unveiled. This person is not afraid to meet the people or to enter a dialogue with them. This person does not consider himself or herself the proprietor of history or of all people, or the liberator of the oppressed; but he or she does commit himself or herself, within history, to fight at their side.

> (p. 39)

We have already introduced notions of research and practice. Transformative practices refer to practices that can disrupt the normal or expected in ways that provide for more powerful learning possibilities for both teachers and students. Transformative, practice-based research involves the questioning and challenging of boundaries that constrain our radical imagination around teaching.

Research is a journey of small steps. Research is painstakingly slow at times, but growth comes and momentum will come your way. What starts as a tweaking of discussion formats for a read aloud may become a school-wide study of "journeys" in literature and life. It is not a journey you can do alone. You need critical friends to collaborate and critique. These friends may come from your own school setting, in graduate school, or in networks of teachers working on the same path. It is a journey that is threatening to some—both colleagues and administrators. It will require that you lead.

Summary

Some teachers believe that the best way to handle oppression from above is to close your door and do what's best for the young people in your classroom. We probably believed that at some point in our own careers. However, there are other ways of dealing with oppression and exploitation in schools and society than closing your door and doing your own thing. What if we opened our doors to our colleagues and asked "what if" questions together? What if we engaged our communities in our search (and research) for more human ways of working with young people? What if we engaged in transformative practices that we study through practice-based research that everyone can take part in and learn from? What if we used practice-based research as a

> ## Points to (Re)Consider
>
> Return to the opening questions. How have your thoughts about yourself as a researcher been affirmed? Challenged? Developed?

leverage for change in our classroom, our school, and our society? We have framed this chapter with *why* questions—Why be a researcher? We hope that our message is clear and that the answer to the question of "Why?" is one that convokes spaces of dialogue, debate, reflection, questioning, and empowerment in your classroom and beyond.

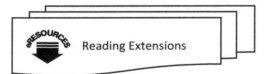

RESOURCES   Reading Extensions

Children's Literature Cited

Tonatiuh, D. (2014). *Separate is never equal: Sylvia Mendez and her family's fight for desegregation*. New York, NY: Harry N. Abrams.

References

Argyris, C., & Schön, D. (1974). *Theory in practice*. San Francisco, CA: Jossey-Bass.

Castoriadis, C. (1997). *World in fragments: Writings on politics, society, psychoanalysis, and the imagination* (D. A. Curtis, Trans. & Ed.). Stanford, CA: Stanford University Press.

Dewey, J. (1964). The child and the curriculum. In R. D. Archambault (Ed.), *John Dewey on education: Selected writings* (pp. 339–358). Chicago, IL: University of Chicago Press.

Duffy, G. G., Miller, S. D., Kear, K., Parsons, S. A., Davis, S. G., & Williams, B. (2008). Teachers' instructional adaptations during reading instruction. In Y. Kim, V. Risko, D. Compton, D. Dickerson, M. Hundley, R. Jimenez, K. Leander, & D. Rowe (Eds.), *57th yearbook of the National Reading Conference* (pp. 160–171). Oak Creek, WI: National Reading Conference.

Freire, P. (1971). *Pedagogy of the oppressed*. New York, NY: Continuum.

Haiven, M., & Khasnabish, A. (2017). *The radical imagination: Social movement research in the age of austerity*. London, UK: Zed Books.

Martinez, M., Stier, C., & Falcon, L. (2016). Judging a book by its cover: An investigation of peritextual features in Caldecott award books. *Children's Literature in Education, 47*(3), 225–241.

Sailors, M. (2019). Re-imagining teacher education. In D. E. Alvermann, N. J. Unrau, M. Sailors, & R. Ruddell (Eds.), *Theoretical models and processes of literacy* (7th ed., pp. 430–448). New York, NY: Routledge.

Schön, D. A. (1983). *The reflective practitioner: How professionals think in action*. New York, NY: Basic Books.

Schön, D. A. (1987). *Educating the reflective practitioner: Toward a new design for teaching and learning in the professions*. San Francisco, CA: Jossey-Bass.

CHAPTER 3

The Roots of Practice-Based Research

Action Research

> **Preview:** In Chapter 2, we started to dig deeply into our teaching practices as central to our work as teachers. Practices refer not just to the range of actions associated with teaching activity but are inclusive of the intentions, thought processes, and disposition to grow practices through reflection. We situated this work as both pragmatic and theoretical in the ways it links emerging personal and community-derived principles of understanding teaching practices. Practice-based research is an approach that is designed to grow our teaching practices into something more powerful. Over the next several chapters, we explore research traditions that have informed our use of the term *practice-based research*. In this chapter, we examine action research as the first of these traditions associated with growing our teaching practices in ways that contribute to societal change.

Imagine this scenario: Entering a few minutes after the first professional development session of the school year had started, Melissa found an empty seat at a table with teachers from her school. "We simply have to do something," one teacher said. "Yes," said the one across the table, "we must take some action against this. We can't ask our children to do this on a daily basis, if at all."

While it's not important (for the sake of this argument) what these teachers were being asked to do (in the name of professional development), what is important is that they were discussing actions to reconcile and remedy that which they found offensive. Defined as the fact or process of doing something, typically to achieve an aim, *action* is a word that has connotations of movement, activity, and doing. While there is a lot of "doing" in many educational research projects, historically it was an "academic researcher" (someone from a

Points to Consider

What is your familiarity with action research? What does it mean to you? What might a teacher do if they were engaged in action research?

university or college) who was doing all the doing, and that doing was to people rather than with people.

This stance toward education research began to shift a bit when, in 1946, Kurt Lewin proposed what he called "action research" in response to his concerns over decontextualized research that relied almost exclusively on statistical methods and experimental designs. Action research was designed to improve communities (for example) by involving the participants in a cyclical process of fact finding, exploratory action, and evaluation. Lewin (1948) framed action research as a paradigm of inquiry where the researcher's primary purpose is to improve the capacity of the community with whom the researcher is working rather than to produce theoretical knowledge. This is not to say that action research cannot contribute to theoretical knowledge. Rather, it is grounded in the context of local goals for improvement.

Connectedness in Action Research

Changing something in the context where it exists is the challenge for the researcher in action research. Changing something in a local context may have effects on things not intended or desired by the researcher. For example, in the fluid context of teaching in classrooms, most everything is connected. A researcher's effort to address one challenge with one change will likely influence other things in the context to change as well. The connecting paths between our actions as teachers and the growth of our students are complex. Sorting through the interactions of motivations, behaviors, identities, and other factors in the context of an action research project is expected and essential to developing a deep understanding of the principles at work.

To illustrate this notion of connectedness, consider a first-grade teacher who is working to address concerns over the decoding skills of her children. She decides to augment her curriculum with an explicit phonics program that she was introduced to in a professional development workshop. She monitors the growth of the use of decoding in her classroom both in isolated phonics assessments and during connected reading. She discovers (and documents) that her children's growth on the isolated skills assessment is accompanied by a lowered interest in reading and decreased use of context clues in connected reading. She does notice, however, that the children are incorporating phonics more as they encode during writing. This is a good example of the connectedness within a context—this teacher noticed that while the program helped her achieve the results she intended (children's decontextualized phonics knowledge increased), this new information did not transfer

Pause and Reflect

Think about the affordances and flexibility that action research offers you as a teacher. How might you use action research to fulfill your goals as a teacher? What are some constraints that you might face? How might you overcome those constraints associated with action research?

to reading within connected text. Interested in the impact the program (and her instruction) was seemingly having on the writing of the children, the teacher took two steps: She revisited the program's impact on motivation to read while continuing to explore how the directedness of the program may have been contributing to the children's growth in writing. Perhaps in a traditional study, the conclusion would have been that the phonics program works in promoting student knowledge of phonics elements, and that would be the end of the study. However, action research allows for flexibility in the focus throughout the study.

Complexity of Practice in Action Research

Similarly, action research recognizes the complexity of practice and the value of the practitioner as the lead in the research effort. Thus, action research works well in classrooms where teachers are exploring their practice, like the first-grade teacher mentioned earlier. It does so because it places as much emphasis on problem posing as integral to research activity as it does on problem solving as the outcome of research. In schools today, the problem posing is typically taken up by those who are not directly engaged in the practice of teaching. These problems are often framed in deficit terms: "We have low comprehension scores on the state examination. What shall we do?" Or, "There is a huge gap in students' vocabulary knowledge between our school and the other schools in our district. What shall we do?" The teacher is positioned as the deliverer of some improved curriculum to address the problem framed by others. In action research, it is the teacher who is responsible for identifying and framing the challenge she will address with her students. It is also the teacher who will frame the research question and the study itself. This is how action research acts to disrupt traditional literacy instruction and research.

To be clear: We are advocates for problem posing as central to action research. However, we believe deficit notions—"What's wrong here and what can we do to 'fix' it?"—pathologize people as well as their language, cultures, and belief systems and are part of larger systems of oppression. To that end, we want to emphasize that action research can (and should) grow out of opportunities and constructivist stances that build on what is there. An asset-based orientation to action research would not look at a teacher's practice as a place to lay blame, but rather would look at the possibilities of practice, specifically focusing on the places of strength, rich in full possibilities. Similarly, action research should also look at assets of teaching practices on which to build. The teacher in the previous example observed something happening in writing that was not intended. This became the basis for a new study. Perhaps a classroom receives access to iPads in support of literacy teaching. Action research could be used to inquire about innovation with this new set of tools in the curriculum.

Pause and Reflect

Action research can and should grow out of opportunities and constructivist stances that build on strengths rather than take a deficit approach ("Let's fix what's wrong"). What are some aspects of your practices that action research might help you reframe toward a more assets-based perspective?

Engaging in Research with Children and Youth

When we engage in culturally sustaining pedagogies, we are

- Recognizing and (re)centering the expertise that young people bring to the classroom that is grounded in their family and community experiences;

- Foregrounding what Ladson-Billings (1995) described as academic success, cultural competence, and sociopolitical consciousness (p. 160); and

- "perpetuat[ing] and foster[ing]—to sustain—linguistic, literate, and cultural pluralism as part of the democratic project of schooling" (Paris, 2012, p. 93).

Action Research as a Focus of Research

Action research has evolved over time in the study of teaching. It became popular in educational circles in the late 20th century and was sometimes called *teacher research*. In their classic 1993 text *Inside/Outside: Teacher Research and Knowledge*, Cochran-Smith and Lytle argued for the importance and potential contributions of teacher research in educational contexts. The increasing attention to action research is seen in the many excellent books on the topic and even a research journal that is focused just on action research studies. To that end, two meta-studies (studies that synthesized findings across individual studies) were conducted that looked at action research; we summarize each in the following section as they stand to inform our understanding of action research.

Features of Action Research

We think the work of Baumann and Hester (2001) is particularly helpful in getting a sense of the features of action research as it was practiced in its earliest days. They conducted a meta-inquiry of studies focused on literacy that adopted a teacher action research framework. They were focused particularly on the methodologies used in these studies. They identified 16 categories that described methodology, which they then classified into four larger groups: (a) general attributes of teacher research, (b) processes of teacher inquiry, (c) teacher research methods, and (d) writing and reporting of classroom inquiry. We briefly summarize their findings around these categories, noting the percentages they report of studies that display these features; we use the terms *action research* and *teacher research* interchangeably in this section.

General Attributes of Teacher Research

All of the studies (100%) were focused on problems teachers face and the questions they pose around these problems. In over half of the studies (59%), the questions in focus tended to change or be modified as the researchers explored their topic. Theory was prominently positioned in the vast majority of the studies. In fact, 97% of the studies were described as "theoretically driven" and 94% were "theoretically productive." Finally, reflection was prominently featured in all of the studies.

Processes of Teacher Inquiry

Ninety-one percent of the studies involved some collaboration among researchers. Researchers described their experiences as creating spaces for them to learn from their students (100%) and also as "clarifying" for them the ways that they make sense of their teaching experiences in the classroom (94%). There were mixed reports on the unsettling or uneasy feelings among the researchers created around the action research work.

Teacher Research Methods

All of the research described researchers' reliance on methods based on practicality and efficiency for addressing the research questions. All of the researchers selected and adapted interpretivist research methods for use in their studies, with some (26%) drawing on post-positivist methods as well.

Writing and Reporting of Classroom Inquiry

In reporting their studies, the researchers tended to rely on narrative forms (94%) such as using excerpts of transcripts or the presentation of work artifacts in their reports. The researchers often relied on vignettes or metaphors to convey key points and ideas.

Although seemingly a bit dated, this report remains important today for several reasons. First, it summarized the status of action research at that point in time, when it was first really starting to take root in the field. As such, it serves to provide a historical context for action research. Second, the ways researchers represented their work remain relevant today as these types of representation (e.g., metaphors and vignettes) support readers of the research reports in making connections to those studies and are thus a form of generalizability. Finally, the process for action research has remained relatively the same since this report was issued.

Action Research in Teacher Education

Often, teachers enrolled in graduate programs are engaged in action research. In fact, in many literacy teacher graduate programs across the country, teachers are required to conduct an action research project as a culminating project in their graduate program. Taking a similar methodological approach to the Baumann and Hester (2001) report, another group of educational researchers (Vaughan & Burnaford, 2016) examined the trends and challenges in teacher education programs in integrating action research into studies. Their meta-study looked at how action research was used in graduate education programs between 2000 and 2015.

Their findings indicate that action research in this context is done with three goals in mind: (a) as a reflective practice; (b) for participatory, critical inquiry; and (c) to effect change in schools and communities as a result of working with teachers as leaders (p. 286). In short, Vaughan and Burnaford showed how (across studies) action research provides teachers with opportunities to grow their attitudes and beliefs in order to develop into reflective and collaborative teacher leaders (p. 286).

As a result of their work, Vaughan and Burnaford (2016) suggested that action research in graduate programs might be used as a conduit between universities (specifically colleges of education) and schools in building bridges between practice and theory. These bridges serve to benefit all learners. Second, they recommended that colleges of education need to unapologetically embrace the worlds of practice and scholarship (Ball & Forzani, 2007) so that the documentation and outcomes of action research inform local policies in schools and districts. Seemingly, colleges of education believe that traditional research should inform policy in schools—so a shift in the perception of action research by colleges of education could contribute to a dialogue about the meaning and contributions of action research to local policies. Finally, members of educational research organizations must engage in and promote the use of university–school partnerships that focus on topics important to practitioners (Lewis, 2009).

Action Research and Teacher Research

The use of the term *teacher research* as rooted in action research made sense as an attempt to take the general principles of action research into classrooms. The problem with this naming as *teacher research* is that the method became identified in terms of who was doing the research, not in terms of what approach was being taken. Teacher research was viewed as something not done by (real?) researchers. Further teacher research was focused on the practical and not the theoretical.

In their work on this topic, Cochran-Smith and Lytle (2009) stepped back from the term *teacher research* to use the term *practitioner research*. They wrote:

> We very intentionally use practitioner research here instead of teacher research, as we did in *Inside/Outside*. We realized many years ago, as we worked with differently positioned educators after the publication of our first book, that the term teacher unnecessarily and inaccurately narrowed the scope of the work. Thus, in this new book, we use practitioners, including teachers to be sure, but also including school and school district administrators . . . teacher candidates, teacher educators. . . [and] others who work inside educational sites of practice.
>
> (p. ix)

Others have used similar terms in an attempt to bring visibility and equality to action research. These terms include *practitioner inquiry*, *practitioner research*, and *teacher inquiry*. Still, criticisms about action research abound: Teachers are not "properly trained" to conduct research, practitioner research is not as rigorous as academic research, and this research is too local and thus not generalizable (Zeichner & Noffke, 2001). Regardless, our use of the term *practice-based research* is designed, in part, to take a stance that research into teaching practices is real (in its focus on practice) and is highly theoretical in its focus on explanation in complexity and the derivation of principles that apply in the moment and possibly in broader contexts.

Action Research and Beyond

There are many excellent books and even journals devoted just to action research (e.g., *Action Research*, *Educational Action Research*, *The Canadian Journal of Action Research*, *Journal of Action Research*, and *The Journal of Teacher Action Research*). And, action research has thrived not only in education but across many other professions. James, Slater, and Buckman (2012) reported a number of variations or derivatives of action research used in other sciences, including action science

(AS), participatory action research (PAR), community-based research (CBR), action learning (AL), appreciative inquiry (AI), living theory (LT), participatory action leadership action research (PALAR), collaborative action research (CAR), and youth participatory action research (YPAR). We address several of these (PAR, CBR, and YPAR) in the next chapter.

Pause and Reflect

What role should the community that your school serves play in an action research project? How might action research be the impetus for a shift in the relationship between the school and its community?

Summary

We have focused this chapter on action research as one of the important research traditions that informs practice-based research. Action research is context-driven and change-oriented. Action research places the practitioner at the center of the research as both the problem poser and problem solver through the use of systematic inquiry. Action

Points to (Re)Consider

What appeals to you about action research? What affordances might it offer a teacher? Go back to the scenario at the opening of the chapter. How might action research help Melissa achieve her goals as a professional?

research is theoretically oriented, even though its focus is on the immediate context for the work. The placement of the practitioner (or practitioners) at the center of the research effort, the focus on taking action to address complex challenges to practice in context, and the focus on theory are features we will bring forward into our representation of practice-based research.

Reading Extensions

References

Allen, J., & Kinloch, V. (2013). Create partnerships, not programs. *Language Arts*, *90*(5), 385–390.

Ball, D. L., & Forzani, F. M. (2007). What makes educational research "educational"? *Educational Researcher*, *36*(9), 529–540.

Baumann, J. F., & Duffy-Hester, A. M. (2001). Making sense of classroom worlds: Methodology in teacher research. In *Methods of literacy research* (pp. 11–32). London: Routledge.

Cochran-Smith, M., & Lytle, S. (2009). *Inquiry as stance: Practitioner research for the next generation*. New York, NY: Teachers College Press.

James, A., Slater, T., & Buckman, A. (2012). *Action research for business, nonprofit and public administration: A tool for complex times*. Los Angeles, CA: Sage.

Ladson-Billings, G. (1995). But that's just good teaching! The case for culturally relevant pedagogy. *Theory Into Practice, 34,* 159–165.

Lewin, K. (1948). *Resolving social conflicts.* New York, NY: Harper.

Lewis, A. (2009). Researching what really works in education. *Phi Delta Kappan, 90*(8), 539–540.

Paris, D. (2012). Culturally sustaining pedagogy: A needed change in stance, terminology, and practice. *Educational Researcher, 41*(3), 93–97.

Vaughan, M., & Burnaford, G. (2016). Action research in graduate teacher education: A review of the literature 2000–2015. *Educational Action Research, 24*(2), 280–299. doi:10.1080/09650792.2015.1062408

Zeichner, K., & Noffke, S. (2001). Practitioner research. In V. Richardson (Ed.), *Handbook of research on teaching* (4th ed., pp. 314–330). Washington, DC: American Educational Research Association.

The Roots of Practice-Based Research

Design-Development Research

Preview: In this chapter, we introduce design-development research as a second tradition associated with growing our teaching practices. Design-development research serves as a complement to action research, introduced in the previous chapter. Unlike in action research, there is no single, historical path for the movement of design-development research into education. In this chapter, we bring together some of the traditions that have informed design-development research and examine its potential for revealing principles of practice and providing us with a mechanism to study them.

Consider this: We are writing this book on a computer that works on an operating system labeled 10.13.6. These numbers reflect the history of development work on this operating system, with each of the three sets of digits, from left to right, representing the relative significance of the changes to the system. Each iteration of the system went through a research and development phase. In part, innovations were made based on challenges or limitations of the previous systems. Other changes may have come based on what competing systems offered, may have been the result of innovations in technology, may have been made based on market considerations, or may have emerged from the imaginative thinking of the developers. The process is iterative. Somewhere, in some research laboratory, there are engineers consulting with marketing staff and salespeople, working on the next version, and at the same time there are additional groups working on an entirely new system.

Points to Consider

What is your familiarity with design-development research? What does it mean to you? What might a teacher do if they were engaged in a design-development research project?

How is research part of this work? Are there theories, principles, questions, data gathering, interpretations, arguments made for each change? The answer is yes. This kind of research is often labeled *applied research*, as traditionally distinguished from *academic* or *basic* research. These distinctions can be helpful, but they can also limit our understanding of research, place restrictions on the use of the scientific method, and create a kind of hierarchy of importance and value for different research approaches. Research and development work on computers, as an example, is both informed by and contributes to propositions such as information theory, programming language theory, artificial intelligence theory, and virtual reality theory. Design and development work on such products are at the center of this kind of activity.

Another familiar space for design–development research is found in formative evaluation. Formative evaluation refers to a process of gathering data to make adjustments in what is being done with the goal of improving productivity. Formative evaluation stands in contrast to summative evaluation. In summative evaluation, data is considered by stakeholders to decide whether to continue or stop doing something altogether. For example, a school district is adopting an SEL (socio-emotional learning) program and plans for three years of implementation. There will be ongoing data collection to monitor implementation as well as effects. Adjustments will be made as challenges are encountered. This is a plan for formative evaluation. At the end of the three-year period, there will likely be a summative evaluation where a final decision will be made to continue or abandon the program. These examples fit into the family of approaches used in design–development research.

Design Research

Design-based research emerged in the 2000s and quickly gained popularity (Anderson & Shattuck, 2012). Ann Brown was a prominent educational psychologist who studied children's learning in the latter half of the 20th century. Many scholars point to the article published by Brown (1992) entitled "Design Experiments: Theoretical and Methodological Challenges in Creating Complex Interventions in Classroom Settings" (along with the work of her associates Collins and Palinscar) as transformative in educational research and seminal in the emergence of a design framework for studying teaching and learning. Brown (1992) explained her approach with a description of her context and her goals:

> The lion's share of my current research program is devoted to the study of learning in the blooming, buzzing confusion of inner-city classrooms. My high-level goal is to transform grade-school classrooms from work sites where students perform assigned tasks under the management of teachers into communities of learning . . . and interpretation . . . where students are given significant opportunity to take charge of their own learning.
>
> (p. 142)

She continued by describing and naming her research approach as design experiments

> modeled on the procedures of the design sciences such as aeronautics and artificial intelligence. As a design scientist in my field, I attempt to engineer innovative educational environments and simultaneously conduct experimental studies of these innovations.
>
> (p. 142)

Brown described her preparation as a classic learning scientist to conduct studies in carefully controlled laboratory settings and her frustration with attempts to take findings from the learning laboratory into classrooms only to meet disappointing results. She summarized her 10 years of work in making connections between laboratory work and classrooms in two seemingly contradictory statements. (1) Training (her words) worked: That is, for children trained to use simple strategies, and when to use them, memory improved. (2) Training didn't work: "There was little evidence of maintenance in the absence of the experimenter's prompting and less evidence of independent transfer" (p. 145).

Brown went on to describe her research with her colleagues in schools working with an approach called "reciprocal teaching." This approach was designed to improve reading comprehension. The methodology focused on four activities that relate to teacher–pupil interactions: questioning, clarifying, summarizing, and predicting. The series of studies on this method became more complex as it was increasingly incorporated into the dynamics of a functioning classroom. Brown's and her colleagues' work concentrated not just on strategies but also on the study of the communities of learning that surrounded the work with these strategies. Brown (1992) described her work in science classrooms where "sixth-, seventh-, and eighth-grade students were responsible for doing collaborative research and sharing their expertise with their colleagues" (p. 149). She insisted that, in order to create a community of learners, it was necessary to set up a classroom ethos that differed from the traditional classroom (p. 149), with a new approach that put the students in control of their learning. Furthermore, Brown believed that positioning the learners in the classroom as inquirers alongside the researchers contributed to the success of the learners learning the strategies.

Brown continued by describing the immense methodological challenges of doing research in these very complex settings. She resisted the quantitative/qualitative distinction for design research, instead stating: "I prefer a mixed approach, suiting the method to the particular data. I mix and match qualitative and quantitative methodologies in order to describe the phenomenon" (p. 156).

Design-Development Research: Naming the Family of Methodologies

The linking of these two terms (*design* and *development*) reflects some of the imprecision in the literature on their use. The field has not always been clear on the distinctions. Anderson and Shattuck (2012) observed that researchers used both terms almost interchangeably. Barab and Squire (2004) offered a similar view in describing educational design research as including "a series of approaches, with the intent of producing new theories, artifacts, and practices that account for and potentially impact learning and teaching in naturalistic settings" (p. 2).

In a 1999 publication, van den Akker et al. referred to this research approach primarily in terms of *development* research. Then, in a 2006 publication, van den Akker, McKenney, Nieveen, and Gravemeijer referred to this research approach primarily in terms of *design* research. In the 2006 study, van den Akker et al. described *design research* as a common label for a family of related research approaches that include

- design studies and design experiments,
- development and development research,
- formative research and formative evaluation, and
- engineering research.

Engaging in Research with Children and Youth

Project-based learning has elements of design principles in it. For example, when young people are designing a bridge that will span a certain area and hold a certain amount of weight, they might be strategic in their attempts. They might design a bridge, test it out, record their findings, and adjust accordingly as they re-test the design. These are elements of design-based research. We can support young people in their efforts by

- Providing spaces and places where they can create and test their designs;
- Providing them with tools to record their attempts (record their data);
- Creating spaces where they think (and act) strategically to modify/adapt their designs and creations; and
- Providing venues where they talk about the development of their design (as well as showing their design).

Richey, Klein, and Nelson (2004) distinguished between Type 1 and Type 2 developmental research. Type 1 development research is highly contextualized and focused on specific product or program design. (This description would apply to the early work of Brown described previously.) The findings and conclusions are very context-specific. Type 2 developmental research is more generalized. (This description would apply to the later stages of Brown's research with reciprocal teaching and the work of others who took up these approaches.) The ultimate goal for this kind of research is the production of knowledge, often in the form of a new design or model, or principles rather than products. In Type 2 research, the researchers may not be involved in the design and development process (including the tools and models applied) in order to come to the conclusions concerning design principles of a more generalizable nature.

Van den Akker, McKenney, Nieveen, and Gravemeijer (2006) built on this distinction when they described the goals as different in their relative contribution to "practice" and "science" as well as the focus on stimulating professional development of participants. This work suggests a difference in design work directed toward more generalizable principles and development work as directed toward improved products and practices. These distinctions should not be considered as a firm dichotomy, as research under either label is both theoretical and practical. The more important distinction is between design-development research that is highly contextualized in practice and traditional educational research that focuses on strategies such as isolation of variables, control of contexts for inquiry, manipulation of single variables while others are held constant, single studies as the important unit of inquiry, and generalizability as essential.

While some might view the plethora of approaches that fall under the design–development umbrella as a signal for lack of rigor, we see these variations as a positive sign of growth. We resist the idea that there is a single definition or way of doing this kind of research, instead seeing the family of approaches as expanding and allowing imagination to flourish. Anderson and Shattuck (2012) examined the use of design–development research in the decade of the 2000s. Using an electronic search focused on the term *design development*, they identified a total of 1,940 articles that discussed the methodology. The rise in publications across the decade expanded steadily, from 0 in the year 2000, to fewer than 50 studies between 2000 and 2003, to over 350 in 2010.

Anderson and Shattuck's (2012) close analysis of 31 studies that used this methodology during this time period revealed that the focus areas were across numerous subjects in education (e.g., mathematics, science, technology, literacy), participants spanned many ages and grade levels (elementary through postsecondary), and both quantitative and qualitative methods were drawn upon. There have been a number of themed journal publications focused on design–development research during the 2000s (e.g., the *Journal of the Learning Sciences*, *13*(1), 2004; *Educational Researcher*, *33*(1), 2003; *Educational Technology*, 2005).

Characteristics of Design-Development Research

Van den Akker et al. (2006) attributed certain characteristics to design–development research. These characteristics are important to consider as we explore the roots of practice-based research. Figure 4.1 summarizes those characteristics; we elaborate in the sections that follow.

Interventionist: the research aims at the study of an intervention in the real world;
Iterative: the research incorporates a cyclic approach to design, evaluation and revision;
Process oriented: no black box model of input-output measurement, the focus in on understanding and improving interventions;
Utility oriented: the merit of a design is measured, in part, by its practicality for users in real contexts; and
Theory oriented: the design is based upon theoretical propositions, and field testing of the design contributes to theory building.

FIGURE 4.1 Characteristics of Design-Development Research

Interventionist

There is a great deal of educational and even classroom research that is observational in nature. The researcher is intentionally not intervening but rather is attempting to understand a phenomenon or a context. This is valuable work, but it does not fall under the design–development framework that involves the researcher making changes. In some ways, the intervention offered is similar to the independent variable in quantitative, experimental research. The researcher manipulates the independent variable (e.g., her questioning strategies) while controlling all of the other variables that might influence the outcome she is interested in affecting. This variable, the dependent variable, is the target for change (e.g., increased reading comprehension abilities). Our claims of cause–effect relationships (e.g., the changes in the questioning strategies led to increased comprehension) rest on careful control of the other variables that might influence outcomes.

In design-development research, there is often less effort in controlling other variables. Dede (2005) asserted that contrary to traditional research methods, in design-development research studies, many variables are deliberately and appropriately not controlled. The "treatment" may evolve considerably over time, and even the research methodologies utilized may shift to fit the changes in the intervention. Researchers allow the context to shift in order to study not just the variable in focus but how the intervention affects other areas. There is, along the lines of most qualitative research, the understanding that what we are studying is connected to everything else. This is one of the great advantages of design-development research. While to some this lack of control of other variables may weaken the argument for simple cause-and-effect relationships between the intervention and the targeted outcome, to others this a strength of this kind of research. The claims that grow out of design-development research are more about the intervention in a context and the changes to the context.

We also want to express some caution about the use of the term *intervention*. There is a decidedly behaviorist and authoritative stance associated with this term. Design-development research is certainly open to more holistic ways of engaging with students in educational experiences. We would encourage you, in your work, to consider alternative terms that are closer to your personal philosophy. For example, you might think in terms of "improvements" that acknowledge the existence of something there, rather than just "intervention." You might think of the intervention as a disruption to the current way of doing something in the classroom that might lead to transformation.

Iterative

One of the most important distinctions between design-development research and other, more traditional forms of intervention research is the changing of the intervention during the research. In traditional research, the intervention (or innovation, or treatment) is fixed and carefully monitored to insure fidelity to the plan. If the intervention is changed, then the findings become invalid and uninterpretable. In design-development research, changes to the intervention are expected. In some cases, the researcher may time these iterations to occur at specific points in the study. Other researchers might be more flexible in deciding when to change the intervention based on the results that might have been observed.

In future chapters, we will examine the work of researchers who make adaptations to the intervention all along the way in their research. These changes are iterative—usually small changes—that grow out of responses observed or not observed and are not completely new approaches. The researcher is careful to document when, how, and why changes are made and to monitor the changes that unfold.

Process Oriented

The design-development researcher is close to practice. There is never just an intervention introduced and then the results assessed at the end. There is always the close and constant inspection of processes associated with the intervention. The data collection and analysis are ongoing during the study. The researcher might be looking at the instructional conversations taking place or documenting the ways in which the student engages with the curriculum.

This kind of process-oriented data collection is used to inform cycles of inquiry and the possible adaptations of the intervention as the study evolves.

Utility Oriented

The design-development researcher is pragmatic, concerned with usefulness and practicality in the context of practice. Traditional instructional research might involve large-scale, well-resourced interventions that are simply not practical or realistic in the contexts in which most teachers work. We see this often in curriculum research that focuses on one segment of the curriculum (e.g., reading instruction) and ignores the other areas. More time, effort, and resources devoted to reading might have positive outcomes, but what is being displaced in the curriculum and at what costs? The design-development researcher is immersed in the context of practice and is careful to assess how interventions introduced into the system fit together with everything else.

Theory Oriented

Theories posit explanations for how things work and why. The term *basic research* is often used to describe studies that test theories. For example, a theory of teacher effectiveness might posit that teacher vocabulary levels (used as a measure for intelligence) are related to the quality of teaching and student learning. A study might investigate whether the prediction of this theory is upheld or not.

While other studies might not test theories, they might adopt a particular theoretical perspective that undergirds the design of their study. For example, a researcher interested in how discourse in a classroom might exclude some students from participation based on race, ethnicity, language, culture, or gender might adopt a critical and sociocultural theoretical frame to ground their study in theory. Design-development research can adopt or situate the work in a particular frame. This kind of theoretical framing is important in making clear the assumptions and perspectives being taken.

Reeves (2006) described the relationship between micro-cycles (the iterative dimension of design research) and theory building from the local, and contrasted traditional research and development-design research. The path for traditional research moves from hypotheses or existing theories, to experiments designed to test the hypotheses, to theories refined based on the findings, and finally to the application of theories to practice. Design research moves from the analysis of problems of practice (problem posing), to the development of solutions based on existing design principles, to iterative cycles of testing and refinement, and finally to the addition

Pause and Reflect

How might the various characteristics of design-development research support you in thinking about your practice? What type of study might you do in your classroom if you were orienting it toward a design-development perspective?

or revision of design principles for work in the area under scrutiny. The theory-building work is sometimes described as the final element of design research, where the researchers step back from the experience of the research (as a retrospective process) to extract design principles.

Design Principles

As Reeves (2006) noted, it is common for researchers who engage in a series of design-development studies around a particular topic to step back and identify a set of principles that seem to be implicated in this work. In our own research into working with preservice teachers, we conducted a series of studies focused on mentoring (or tutoring) as a potentially powerful context for learning to teach literacy. We situated mentoring as a "hybrid space" where preservice teachers have the experience of exploring practices in real teaching contexts that don't have all of the conditions of teaching in classrooms. This research involved multiple studies following the design-research approach. We have stepped back from this work to infer the qualities or design principles associated with quality mentoring/tutoring of young students (see Figure 4.2). Classroom teachers are used to having students pulled out of their classroom for "tutoring." It might be beneficial to examine these tutorial experiences in consideration of the design principles we have identified. Could the discrepancies become the basis for a practice-based research study?

Offer a combination of work in a predictable structure (i.e., models and expectations for work in certain areas and methods) and in flexible spaces where you can be responsive to the child in the moment.
Insure ample time in sessions over an extended period to encourage relationship building and insure deep engagement with content.
Create spaces for exploring multi-model forms of literacy that engage the child in both reading and composing texts.
Employ assessment practices that are appreciative of; build on, and responsive to the resources the child brings to the tutoring/mentoring context.
Follow the child's lead in developing the curriculum based on interests.
Focus on identity building ("I am a reader who. . . ").
Encourage reflection throughout the experience.
Promote a community of practice with children working with each other.
Be explicit in your work with strategies that support reading development.
Personalize everything with the child. (e.g., I brought this book for you today because . . .)
Learn and grow with the child. What are they teaching you?
Offer choices whenever possible.
Engage with materials that are culturally relevant in culturally sustaining frameworks.
Connect work in literacy to work in the classroom and literacy experiences at home.
Document accomplishments in the text environment you create and take time to celebrate.

FIGURE 4.2 Design Principles for Tutoring/Mentoring Programs in Support of Literacy

Generalizability

Researchers who take a post-positivist perspective on research would often like to generalize the findings from their research to others in similar contexts. A post-positivist study of second graders examining the effects of vocabulary study on reading comprehension would like to argue that the findings are relevant to all second graders working under similar conditions. Technically, inferences like this are limited to the population sampled, but the research might argue that the findings are more broadly relevant. At some point, the generalizability of the findings comes into question—just second graders? All elementary students?

Researchers who take a more interpretivist perspective are reluctant to make inferences beyond who was studied, when, and by whom. At best, interpretivist researchers will provide enough detail on their work that others who want to draw on those findings can make the necessary connections.

Most design-development researchers stand on the side of interpretivist research on this issue. They are reluctant to make claims that go beyond the group they have studied. This limitation does not make their research any less valuable or valid. It just makes it different in the ways it contributes to the topic in the literature.

Challenges

Despite the numerous articles extolling the benefits of design-development research, there have also been a number of useful critiques—notably Barab and Squire's (2004) article. They argued that "if a researcher is intimately involved in the conceptualization, design, development, implementation, and researching of a pedagogical approach, then ensuring that researchers can make credible and trustworthy assertions is a challenge" (p. 10). This challenge is a familiar one to anthropological and many forms of interpretivist research in that none of these methods can or does claim that the researcher's bias is removed from the research process. Indeed, some interpretivist proponents argue that the researchers themselves (with their biases, insights, and deep understanding of the context) are the best research tool.

Summary

There are clear common features to the two approaches introduced in this chapter and in the previous chapter on action research (e.g., context matters). There are differences as well (e.g., the importance of the researcher as insider to the practice). It is not unusual at all for researchers to describe their approach to research as drawing on traditions from action research and design-development research. Cole, Purao, Rossi, and Sein (2005) argued that both of these methodologies share a common "meta-paradigm"—pragmatism.

Practitioners who read about these methodologies might com-

Points to (Re)Consider

What appeals to you about action research? What affordances might it offer a teacher? What do you see as its benefits to teachers? Limitations? Challenges?

ment: Isn't this just like what teachers do all the time as they grow their practices? The answer is yes. Framing this as research, however, places an additional set of requirements that many teachers don't often include as they are only working toward developing their own understanding—not attempting to convince others and the field that the principles they have explored are deserving of broader attention.

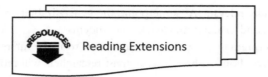

Reading Extensions

References

Anderson, T., & Shattuck, J. (2012). Design-based research: A decade of progress in education research? *Educational Researcher, 41*(1), 16–25.

Barab, S., & Squire, K. (2004). Design-based research: Putting a stake in the ground. *Journal of the Learning Sciences, 13*(1), 1–14.

Brown, A. (1992). Design experiments: Theoretical and methodological challenges in creating complex interventions in classroom settings. *Journal of the Learning Sciences, 2*(2), 141–178.

Cole, R., Purao, S., Rossi, M., & Sein, M. K. (2005). Being proactive: Where action research meets design research. In D. Avison, D. Galletta, & J. I. DeGross (Eds.), *ICIS international conference on information systems, Las Vegas, USA, December 11–14, 2005* (pp. 325–335). Las Vegas, NV: Association for Information Systems.

Dede, C. (2005). Why design-based research is both important and difficult. *Educational Technology, 45*(1), 5–8.

Reeves, T. C. (2006). Design research from a technology perspective. In J. Van den Akker, K. Gravemeijer, S. McKenney, & N. Nieveen (Eds.), *Educational design research* (pp. 52–66). London: Routledge.

Richey, R. C., Klein, J. D., & Nelson, W. A. (2004). Developmental research: Studies of instructional design and development. In D. H. Jonassen (Ed.), *Handbook of research for educational communications and technology* (pp. 1099–1130). Mahwah, NJ: Lawrence Erlbaum Associates.

van den Akker, J., McKenney, S., Nieveen, N. M., & Gravemeijer, K. (2006). Introducing educational design research. In J. van den Akker, K. Gravemeijer, S. McKenney, & N. Nieveen (Eds.), *Educational design research* (pp. 3–7). London, UK: Routledge.

The Roots of Practice-Based Research

Transformative Research

Preview: In this chapter, we introduce transformative research as a third research tradition that informs our work in practice-based research. Transformative research is less about the method and more about the processes of and goals for research. Transformative research assumes an activist stance where research is used as a tool for social change and social justice.

Imagine this scenario: Two researchers walk into a staff meeting at a local school. Their study was recently approved by their local institutional review board (IRB) and they are excited to "pitch" the study to the teachers on this campus. As they begin their presentation about the study, they tell the teachers what they've identified as the problem the school faces (probably something that has to do with achievement scores), what the literature says about the problem (probably identifies some "best practice" that will raise scores), and what they want to study (probably the effects of some innovative curriculum or prac-

Points to Consider

What is your stance toward the role of research in social change? Under what conditions/context do researchers have an ethical and moral obligation to contribute to the social "good"?

tice). It's at that point that the two researchers invite the teachers and their children and youth to be "subjects" in their study. You could almost have heard the crossing of the teachers' arms at the mention of the word, "subject." After all, who wants to be "subjected" to a "treatment"?

While this scenario may be a bit contrived (most academics who engage in school-based research prefer the term *participate*), we still find people being referred to as *subjects* in academic spaces. Sometimes it's the word that IRB uses, sometimes journals publish studies that use the word, and frankly, sometimes we hear other educational researchers use the word. That is not our stance and that is not a stance that is in keeping with the focus of this chapter: practice-based research. In fact, it's difficult to imagine a teacher who does practice-based research talking about their participants (young people in their classroom) as "subjects."

It was not that long ago that most research reports in social science journals used the term *subjects* to describe the individuals who participated in a study. In the 1994 edition of the American Psychological Association (APA) style manual, there was a first-time recommendation for the use of the term *participants* over *subjects* in the reporting of research. In part, this shift recognized the increasing recognition of the treatment of participants as individuals, with a constant consideration of their rights. In part, this shift acknowledged that research involving humans must recognize and be responsive to this kind of research as engaging with humans. The debates over the use of the term *participants* are still not settled. While some object to its use because it suggests a lack of agency on the part of the people who are in the study, the shift has become common in research reporting—with the caveat that APA guidelines still leave open the choice of terms. The way we position people who engage with us in our research is also reminiscent of how we position them, their knowledge and expertise, and their abilities to identify and solve problems within their communities. Words are important, and how we talk to, with, and about people in research studies stands to inform how we engage with them.

We open this chapter with a consideration of how we use words to describe others in our research because it points to research that engages with people as relational. Humanizing research is important to us and important to our commitments to practice-based research. We simply can't imagine a practice-based research study in which there is not deep engagement with the participants that starts with respect and an invitation to the role as co-researcher. For us, the growth of transformative research—the focus of this chapter—is tied to the very notion of research as humanizing. Transformative research is the third root that we draw upon in creating an argument for practice-based research.

Ways of Thinking About Transformative Research

Mertens (2019) wrote about transformative research as a research paradigm. In framing her book on educational research methods, Mertens distinguished between several different and broad paradigms for research. One of these paradigms she labeled as "transformative." At the center of transformative research is the promotion of human rights and an increase in social justice. Transformative research recognizes that there are various versions of reality and those realities are based on the way society privileges people, languages, and cultures. Transformative research methods are heavily influenced by the theories that guide the research. However, the approaches share (a) a focus on the human condition, including the humanity of the researcher; (b) a focus on something in a context that is oppressive to individuals or to a society; and (c) the researcher taking action in a study—engaging with other humans—to confront these issues and disrupt the status quo. From this perspective, the researcher is not (and cannot be) neutral or distant. Rather, the researcher is present, active, and committed. And, the researcher takes on a political stance by their presence in the research space. While some might describe this kind of work as (just) activism, we (and others) see this as research plus activism as there is systematic research taking place alongside activism. In so many ways, this is activist research—the researcher is taking on the work purposefully, in collegial ways with the people in that shared space, gathering and analyzing data, and using the findings for social change.

Over time, transformative research has instantiated in several different ways, including participatory action research, community-based research, and youth participatory action research. Each of these three types of research is held together by the emancipatory stance the researcher and research team take toward their work. While we hesitate to summarize, at the risk of oversimplifying these research methods, we briefly describe each of them here in terms of how they contribute to practice-based research.

Participatory Action Research

Perhaps of the three we present here, *participatory action research* (PAR) is one of the oldest, drawing directly from the action research movement of the 1940s. However, one of the most critical differences between action research and PAR is the shaping of PAR by other intellectual work, including various types of feminism, Marxism, critical race theory, emancipatory traditions, and liberatory traditions. Researchers who engage in PAR focus their attention on how research can be used to re-center the everyday experiences and expertise of people, especially those who are marginalized by society, into that of conscious building, from a Freirean perspective. Many of the methods used in PAR were developed by local people, not academics, in countries that were seeking social and political liberation from colonizing powers (Mirra, Garcia, & Morrell, 2015) through revolution (such as Brazil, Cuba, and Nicaragua). Literacy campaigns were at the heart of these endeavors and PAR played a significant role in bridging the two.

Because of its heavy reliance on the mutuality between theory and practice (Jordan, 2008), teams that use PAR tend to distance themselves from post-positivist research methods. The belief is that post-positivist research methods are colonial in nature, and those methods reproduce cultural imperialism, where one culture dominates another through the methods. Think in terms of the rigidness of post-positivist research methods. For example, in post-positivist research, the researcher must maintain a personal/professional distance from the participants; otherwise, claims of undue influence over data collection and analysis can be made. Likewise, a researcher using post-positivist methods would use a properly validated and reliable instrument to "capture" data. (See how colonial that sounds?) This flies in the face of the more humanizing methods used in PAR. PAR methods are all about the relationship the researcher has with the people they are working with. Cold, distant instruments that take very little of people's humanity into consideration are outside of the norms of PAR methods. PAR studies tend to be small and local and thus resistant to the colonial practices of many "outside" researchers.

For teachers who are interested in using PAR methods, we offer one caution: Teachers (as other researchers) are often positioned as "experts," sanctioned by our roles and the way people position us as professional. As such, it will be difficult to disrupt the inherent issues of power and authority you have through that role and the way you are positioned. The mere act of participation in a PAR

Pause and Reflect

Schools are institutions within our society. What are some of the artifacts, cultures, and traditions of the institution of school? What are some other institutions that come into contact with schools? What are the artifacts, cultures, and traditions of those institutions?

study—or a practice-based research study that grows out of the spirit of PAR—does not equalize participation, nor does it erase power. Equalizing power, authority, and expertise in a PAR study is critical, and it can be done. Researchers have to be cognizant and constantly aware of their inherent power inside their research relationships and actively disrupt it.

Community-Based Action Research

Growing out of Lewin's work in action research, a community-based collaborative approach to research that involves "stakeholders" in communities is known as *community-based action research* (CBAR). Sometimes called *community action research*, CBAR creates research partnerships and alliances with community stakeholders to explore and develop solutions to local problems, concerns, and challenges. It orients around an issue or strategies and then produces analysis that informs action. As such, it is both community-based and place-based, focusing on geographical places such as neighborhoods.

Traditional models of community-based work (development work and research) have a long line of intrusive "interventionist" approaches where the researcher and their team enter into a community, tell them what's "wrong," and "intervene" to "fix the problem." Often, "interventions" that come into communities (from outsiders) have disappointing results because the complex social concerns of communities are difficult for outsiders to understand. Insiders, or community members, deeply understand and can identify challenges their community faces. Those same community members often have the expertise to solve those challenges. Over centuries and across communities and countries, this type of research quite often pathologized people's cultural and linguistic practices, centering Western/Northern notions and ideologies as that which is "good" and "proper" over local knowledge and expertise. CBAR counters those methods and, instead, relies heavily on the research that is already underway in community-based, social movements.

The core principles of CBAR orient around ensuring that community members participate not only in the research (identifying challenges, developing outcomes) but also in the researching process. Often interviews, focus groups, and what's called "community-engaged mapping," or "asset mapping," are ways to identify local cultural "assets" in the community—local people, organizations, facilities, and businesses who can participate in the community-based action research project. These data sources ensure that the perspectives and experiences of the people who live in the place of the research are well represented throughout the process.

In education, university partnerships are often built on notions of CBAR. The work of Campano, Ghiso, and Welch (2015) is a good example of the use of CBAR to redistribute knowledge wealth. In their work, the team explored and outlined a set of ethical and professional guidelines in community-based research, describing principles that foster "trust within contexts of cultural diversity, systemic inequity, and power asymmetry" (p. 30). First, they argued, equality is the starting point, not the end point. Second, they said that community members' knowledge and perspectives must be taken seriously. Third, they insisted that specific research foci and questions be co-designed with community members. And, while the action research that a teacher might do may not directly involve the community, the point of CBAR is very similar to that of action research (or teacher research, whichever you prefer to call it): dismantling existing hierarchies of knowledge production.

Youth Participatory Action Research

The third tradition in transformative research that has influenced our thinking about practice-based research is known as youth participatory action research (YPAR). YPAR grew out of action research and participatory action research and is also driven by critical theories; it shares many values and goals with PAR and recognizes youth as intellectual beings in and of their own right, with the ability to engage in critical investigations of community issues. Likewise, YPAR recognizes the ability of youth to produce knowledge that can be used to right the inequities in our society. Most often, this research is done in classrooms by teachers, youth, and researchers. YPAR and the pedagogical practices that surround it support youth in understanding and acting upon the social, economic, and historical inequities that have shaped society's oppression of them.

Engaging in Research with Children and Youth

When used as a pedagogical tool, youth participatory action research (YPAR) can create spaces where youth critically analyze the structural inequalities in schools and society (Cammarota, 2008). In order to systematically include it as part of your curriculum and instruction, you might

- Attend to the four-entry points Caraballo, Lozenski, Lyiscott, and Morrell (2017) found in their review of studies;

- Recognize that children and youth already engage in research within their communities (from an assets-based perspective) and begin there while engaging them in school-based research practices; and

- Advocate for the inclusion of YPAR in your school's curriculum.

Drawing heavily from a Freirean perspective (Morrell, 2006), YPAR recognizes that, in order for people to liberate themselves, they must first recognize the root causes of the oppression so that they can create new situations through the use of their radical imagination and civic action. McIntyre (2000) argued for the power of "engaging in a process that positions youth as agents of inquiry and as 'experts' about their own lives" (p. 126). This was a shift toward drawing on epistemologies of resistance with young people, the very people who are most affected by inequities in schools. This shift toward using research with youth as a pedagogical tool took on what Freire (1970) called "problem-posing education." From this stance, teachers and learners embark on a learning journey together—both with expertise that stands to inform the other.

Often using counternarratives to dispel widely held beliefs about children and youth of color (Kirshner & Pozzoboni, 2011), YPAR studies highlight the voices of youth typically silenced in communities (Quijada Cerecer, Cahill, & Bradley, 2011). When used as a pedagogical tool, YPAR can create spaces where historically marginalized youth critically analyze the structural inequalities in schools and society (Cammarota, 2008). When engaged in YPAR, children and youth engage in a critical cycle of inquiry: They identify the research issue, they gather data on the issue, they analyze the data, and they develop and enact an action plan. And, they study the impact of the action on their community.

Recently, Caraballo et al. (2017) conducted a review of PAR and YPAR studies appearing in the literature. They found four entry points that indicate how youth researchers and adult co-researchers conceptualized YPAR in their work. The first entry point was through academic learning and literacies. That is, by its very nature, YPAR provides youth access to—and positions them as critical producers of—complex thinking skills and strategies. Pedagogies that engage youth in YPAR are doing so in ways that counter deficit notions of youth and engage them as intellectual beings. As a result, Morrell (2004) found that youth take on identities as critical researchers and develop activist dispositions.

The second entry point was through cultural and critical epistemological research. As such, YPAR provides a way for youth to reclaim their heritage and identity and counter the "melting pot" assimilationist view taken on so long by society (Caraballo et al., 2017).

The third entry point was through youth development and leadership, most notably the social and emotional development that takes place through the process of research. This, according to Caraballo et al. (2017), provides youth the "capacity and hope to withstand and transform inequitable educational environments" (p. 321).

The fourth entry point was through youth organizing and civic engagement. Youth, through YPAR experiences, have informed policy and practice on local scales, including issues related to school closings, language rights, gendered bathrooms (p. 322), and most recently, gun violence. YPAR experiences provide a pathway for youth to gain organizational skills.

Although YPAR looks methodologically very similar to action research, PAR, and CBR, its main difference is that it involves critical praxis. Duncan-Andrade and Morrell (2008) described what they called a "cycle of praxis" that involved youth

> (1) identify[ing] a problem, (2) research[ing] the problem, (3) develop[ing] a collective plan of action to address the problem, (4) implement[ing] the collective plan of action, and (5) evaluat[ing] the action, assess[ing] its efficacy, and re-exam[ing] the state of the problem.
>
> (p. 12)

It is important to note that the cycle begins with the identification of a problem by the youth. The role of the teacher is to facilitate the process and act as a co-researcher/co-collaborator with the youth. This requires that teachers take on a stance toward their teaching that is very different from modern models of teaching.

In fact, when teachers engage their youth in YPAR, they move into spaces that disrupt traditional practices. In some cases, engaging in YPAR with youth moves teachers toward more humanizing interactions with children and youth. For example, studies have documented shifts in teacher perception of youth,

Pause and Reflect

If you are not already engaging your children or youth in youth participatory action research (YPAR), how might you create spaces in your curriculum where YPAR finds a space? What would you need to do in order to create those spaces? How can you involve your children and youth in decisions about doing YPAR?

especially when their work with youth creates an environment where they (the teachers) shift their curriculum to be inclusive of the digital literacies that their youth use as activists (Kamler & Comber, 2005). Similarly, preservice teachers, too, are influenced by YPAR with their youth. For example, Morrell and Collatos's (2002) work in Los Angeles showed what authentic communities of practice might look like when preservice teachers and youth worked together as "coparticipants" in research (p. 68).

This is a short description of the ways in which teachers are influenced by their children's participation in YPAR. We provide a fuller overview of this research in Chapter 6.

The Role of the Radical Imagination in Transformative Research

Our imagination allows us to engage in realities that cannot be captured through our senses alone. But, that's not to say that lived experiences (and those that we encounter vicariously) do not influence our imagination—they do. In fact, there is a recursive cycle between our lived experiences and our imaginings, and that circular nature deepens our perceptions (Dewey, 1934). Furthermore, our imagination does not exist only inside our head, as has been traditionally thought of and talked about. On the contrary, our imagination is formed within a social context, alongside and with other people's imaginations. These "shared imaginaries" are "landscapes of shared understandings and narratives" (Haiven & Kasnabish, 2017, p. 5) that make it possible for us to live together, to share goals, and to transform our society.

As such, our imagination is the way our experience is broadened because "[we] can imagine what [we] have not seen, can conceptualize something from another person's narration and description of what [we ourselves] ha[ve] never experienced" (Vygotsky, 2004, p. 17). In so many ways, our imagination allows us to "create an infinite number of alternative and past realities" (Lyons, 2005, p. 21). It is through our imagination that we can envision a different reality for today and for tomorrow. It is in this spirit that we now turn our attention to what is called our *radical imagination*. Our radical imagination (accessing it, developing it, and sharing it) becomes the critical component in social change.

What is the "Radical Imagination"?

Social change can only take place in the presence of people (especially teachers) who understand, are aware of, and actively recognize that social inequities exist. That is, the issues we face as a society—issues that are political and economic in nature—are a result of deeply and historically rooted tensions, contradictions, imbalances of power, and forms of oppression and exploitation in our society. Every society institutes itself through its norms, values, language(s), tools, procedures, and methods of "doing" daily life. But, these norms, values, language(s), tools, procedures, and methods are not given to us by the natural world. Rather, they are all social constructs, invented by people, for people. And, those constructs are only as powerful as we, as a society, allow them to be.

In fact, Castoriadis (Rosengren, 2014) used the metaphor of magma to represent social institutions, how they are formed, and how they are maintained. Magma is the moving blend of molten or semi-molten rock. Sometimes magma contains crystals, dissolved gases, and gas bubbles, which can represent the artifacts, cultures, and traditions of institutions. Magma takes on the shape of the space it moves through as it flows downstream, sometimes taking over that space. And, as it moves downstream, magma is making a world (think about the growth that takes place, over time, after a lava flow and the rich, fertile ground that is a result of that flow).

Because humans are in a constant state of making sense of their world while they are making their world, humans are always, as Castoriadis described, moving "downstream." As a concept, the metaphor illustrates a world that is in the process of being made, rather than one that is already made. This person-made world, for many, appears to exist as a result of the natural world; part of this is because we belong to what Anzaldúa (2015) called a "consensual" reality (p. 45), one that we, as a society, have collectively agreed to. Some would call this the status quo ("It is what it is"), and many people feel reality cannot be changed. With that attitude come silence and complacency. Our silence and complacency yield what have been called spectators and accomplices (King, 2016) in the consensual reality.

More recently, scholars have written about the radical imagination as having the potential to transform "self, consciousness, community, culture, society" (Anzaldúa, 2015, p. 44) through a reexamination of "persistent problems that impede efforts at social transformation" (Strasinger, 2010, p. 91). Our radical imagination allows us to "first visualize and then materialize that which does not exist" (Strasinger, 2010, p. 91), such as what we want our tomorrow to look like as well as our today. However, in that visualizing, it is important to not just try to find alternatives to today. These alternatives, called "counterstances" by Anzaldúa (2007, p. 100), are reactions to the values and beliefs of the dominant culture. Perhaps this is why teachers (and others who are engaged in social activism) become frustrated with disruptions. They are locked into what Anzaldúa (2007) described as a "dual between the oppressor and oppressed" (p. 100).

But, the consensual reality can be revised. Metaphorically, Castoriadis noted that magma also represents change in our society. Like magma, changes often lead to instability, volatility, and destructive outbreaks, and the cooling down and formation of new ground is how institutions in our societies are developed through the change process. To fully tap into our radical imagination is to allow ourselves to reach a new consciousness, one that allows us to "suspend the conscious 'I' that reminds [us] of our history and [our] beliefs because these reminders tie [us] to certain notions of reality and

Pause and Reflect

What are some aspects of the institution of school (and education, writ large) that belong to our consensual reality (Anzaldúa, 2015)? Which of those aspects do most people believe cannot be changed? How are you (and other teachers) complacent or silent about those aspects? How can we engage our radical imaginations to address those aspects of our consensual reality?

behavior" (Anzaldúa, 2015, p. 44). In order to break away from reality (and counterstances), Anzaldúa (2015) said we must "insert the idea, with accompanying images of the new reality. To invent this new reality, you cultivate a pretend reality and act as though you're already in that pretend reality. Eventually that reality becomes the real one, at least until you change it again" (p. 44).

How Do We Access and Build it With Teachers? The Role of Research

We ascribe to the notion that we all must engage in our radical imagination so that all people can realize their potential, for as long as there are oppressed, no one is realizing their full humanity (Freire, 1970). So, how do we build these collectives around ourselves as teachers so that we create spaces where the children and youth with whom we work can engage in their radical imagination? To be clear: YPAR and other pedagogical practices similar to it are doing just that—accessing and developing the radical imagination of youth who work with them. But what about building the radical imagination of teachers? In other places, we have illustrated not only the importance of the radical imagination to teacher education but the lack of attention it gets in theories of teacher education (Sailors, 2019). Others have also demonstrated that imagination is only given a cursory glance in education (Heath, 2008) and that the model of imagination that the field relies upon is one that draws from what we have seen or done (p. 120). However, if teachers are going to participate in the social movement of righting the inequities and injustices inside the institution of school, they, too, must engage in their radical imagination. While there are many ways to access and grow the radical imagination of both preservice and in-service teachers (Sailors, 2019), we center our discussion here on the role of research in doing so.

We rely heavily on the work of Haiven and Kasnabish (2010, 2017) in thinking about connecting the radical imagination to practice-based research. They (2017) offer three ways of thinking about the role of researchers in social movements:

- Researchers can invoke research methods, which mobilizes the researcher into the movement.
- Researchers can pass power to the movement through teaching the members research methods, and the researcher would retreat into the movement.
- Researchers can convoke, through participation with members of the movement, spaces of dialogue, debate, reflection, questioning, and empowerment.

(p. 17)

This notion of convocation puts the privilege and power into the hands of the movement. This is a radical call for teachers (as members of the social movement) to actively engage in research, research that is grounded in their day-to-day practices—research that involves their children and youth as co-conspirators in the movement. This requires that we, as teachers and teacher educators, be aware of our participation in consensual reality (Anzaldúa, 2015) and that we are prepared to engage with our radical imagination for social change. This also requires that we not simply reject and "push back" on imposing practices that intrude into the classroom space or engage in counterstances (Anzaldúa, 2007). Rather, we must find a way to ask questions that bring us into a new reality, one that only our radical imagination can move us into. Together we could reimagine research as part of an evolving social process, one in which the teacher educator/researcher convenes and convokes the social processes of research (Haiven & Khasnabish, 2017).

Summary

The addition of transformative research to action research and design-development research as the basis for practice-based research calls attention to the social context for the work we do in promoting education as a pathway for our graduates in transforming the society they will inherit. We recognize that the degree to which practice-based research is enacted from a transformational stance can vary enormously. Practice-based literacy research, for example, that strives to put meaning in the foreground of all teaching and pushes against a commodified, reductionist curriculum that focuses on isolated skills, is transformative in

Points to (Re)Consider

Return to the opening question: Are there any aspects of your response that you are rethinking? What role does practice-based research play in radically reimagining a better today and tomorrow?

the sense that it disrupts banking education models (following Freire) as the normal. Further along the continuum of transformative research is practice-based research that intentionally disrupts, for example, institutional structures (e.g., grouping and tracking plans) that privilege the privileged and penalize the penalized. The other examples in this chapter illustrate even more radical approaches and topics related to transformative research.

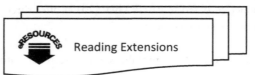

Reading Extensions

References

Anzaldúa, G. (2007). *Borderlands/La frontera* (3rd ed.). San Francisco, CA: Aunt Lute Books.

Anzaldúa, G. (2015). *Light in the dark: Luz en lo oscuro: Rewriting identity, spirituality, reality.* Durham, NC: Duke University Press.

Cammarota, J. (2008). The cultural organizing of youth ethnographers: Formalizing a praxis-based pedagogy. *Anthropology & Education Quarterly, 39*(1), 45–58.

Campano, G., Ghiso, M. P., & Welch, B. J. (2015). Ethical and professional norms in community-based research. *Harvard Educational Review, 85*(1), 29–49.

Caraballo, L., Lozenski, B. D., Lyiscott, J. J., & Morrell, E. (2017). YPAR and critical epistemologies: Rethinking education research. *Review of Research in Education, 41*(1), 311–336.

Dewey, J. (1934). *Art as experience.* New York, NY: Perigee Book.

Duncan-Andrade, J. M., & Morrell, E. (2008). *The art of critical pedagogy.* New York, NY: Peter Lang.

Freire, P. (1970). *Pedagogy of the oppressed.* New York, NY: Continuum.

Haiven, M., & Khasnabish, A. (2010). What is radical imagination? [Special issue]. *Affinities: A Journal of Radical Theory, Culture, and Action, 4*(2), I-XXXVII.

Haiven, M., & Khasnabish, A. (2017). *The radical imagination: Social movement research in the age of austerity.* London, UK: Zed Books.

Heath, G. (2008). Exploring the imagination to establish frameworks for learning. *Studies in Philosophical Education, 27*, 115–123.

Jordan, S. (2008). Participatory action research. In L. M. Given (Ed.), *The Sage encyclopedia of qualitative research methods* (pp. 601–605). Los Angeles, CA: Sage.

Kamler, B., & Comber, B. (2005). Designing turn-around pedagogies and contesting deficit assumptions. In B. Comber & B. Kamler (Eds.), *Turn-around pedagogies: Literacy interventions for at-risk students* (pp. 1–13). Newtown, NSW: Primary English Teaching Association.

King, J. E. (2016). We may well become accomplices: To rear a generation of specaturos is not to educate at all. *Educational Researcher, 45*(2), 159–172.

Kirshner, B., & Pozzoboni, K. (2011). Student interpretations of a school closure: Implications for student voice in equity-based school reform. *Teachers College Record, 113*(8), 1633–1667.

Lyons, J. D. (2005). *Before imagination: Embodied thought from Montaigne to Rousseau*. Stanford, CA: Stanford University Press.

Mcintyre, A. (2000). Constructing meaning about violence, school, and community: Participatory action research with urban youth. *Urban Review, 32*(2), 123–154.

Mertens, M. (2019). *Research and evaluation in education and psychology: Integrating diversity with quantitative, qualitative, and mixed methods* (5th ed.). New York, NY: Sage.

Mirra, N., Garcia, A., & Morrell, N. (2015). *Doing youth participatory action research: Transforming inquiry with researchers, educators, and students*. New York, NY: Routledge.

Morrell, E. (2004). *Becoming critical researchers: Literacy and empowerment of urban youth*. New York, NY: Peter Lang.

Morrell, E. (2006). Critical participatory action research and the literacy achievement of ethnic minority groups. In J.V. Hoffman, D. L. Schallert, C. M. Fairbanks, J. Worthy, & B. Maloda (Eds.), *55th yearbook of the National Reading Conference* (pp. 1–18). Oak Creek, WI: National Reading Conference.

Morrell, E., & Collatos, A. (2002). Toward a critical teacher education: High school student sociologists as teacher educators. *Social Justice, 29*(4), 60–70.

Quijada Cerecer, D. A., Cahill, C., & Bradley, M. (2011). Resist this! Embodying the contradictory positions and collective possibilities of transformative resistance. *International Journal of Qualitative Studies in Education, 24*(5), 587–593.

Rosengren, M. (2014). Magma. In S. Adams (Ed.), *Cornelius Castoriadis key concepts* (pp. 65–74). New York, NY: Bloomsbury.

Sailors, M. (2019). Re-imagining teacher education. In D. E. Alvermann, N. J. Unrau, M. Sailors, & R. Ruddell (Eds.), *Theoretical models and processes of literacy* (7th ed., pp. 430–448). New York, NY: Routledge.

Strasinger, R. (2010). Beyond protest: Radical imagination and the global justice movement. *Affinities: A Journal of Radical Theory, Culture, and Action, 4*(2), 84–106.

Vygotsky, L. S. (2004). Imagination and creativity in childhood. *Journal of Russian and East European Psychology, 42*(1), 7–97.

6 Drawing Between and Across Practice-Based Research

Preview: In this chapter, we formalize our use of the term practice-based research and commit to a set of features that defines this work. We begin by positioning practice-based research in relation to other approaches used generally in educational research. We do not argue that practice-based research is better, more (or less) theoretical, more (or less) rigorous, or more (or less) important than other forms of educational research. We do argue that practice-based research opens our profession up to a different set of tools, a different set of perspectives, a different set of questions, and a different set of potential contributions to both the improvement of literacy teaching and the professionalization of teaching as a practice.

Imagine this scenario: You enter into a space of research (in a course at your local university, or in a professional learning space with other teachers, for example) and are asked to describe your research interests. The very first person to introduce themselves says they are a "quantitative" person. Someone else introduces themselves as a "qualitative" person. You have no idea what side you are supposed to take, nor even if you must.

We have explored in previous chapters the relationship between scientific thinking (reflection) and the scientific method. In both of

Points to Consider

If someone were to ask you the question: "What are you? Are you a quantitative researcher or a qualitative researcher?" How would you respond? Do you think the distinction is important?

these, we found consensus around the activities of framing questions, gathering empirical evidence, interpreting findings, making arguments for the significance of a contribution to the area of study, and placing this work in the hands of a community of peers for independent evaluation. It comes as no surprise that there is enormous variability in the actual approaches used in research studies. Some of this variability is based on different views of knowledge and the world as assumed by the researcher (epistemological), some is the result of different subject areas and contexts of inquiry and the traditions that are shared by different groups of researchers (paradigmatic), some is the result of different kinds of questions being asked, and some has to do with the emergence of new approaches to research.

While many researchers tend to work within a single paradigm or research approach, this is not always the case. The choice of how a researcher engages in inquiry is for the researcher to determine. Many researchers move flexibly between approaches in their work as a function of their questions and context.

Paradigm Wars

While we are advocates for the growing flexibility and variability in the various forms of research, there are researchers who are concerned by it. These scientists hold fast to a traditional view that only one approach (theirs) counts as "real" research. Or, they might suggest that there is a hierarchy of value; some approaches may be useful in some exploratory sense, but at the top of the scale of research approaches there is one that matters most. This notion is reinforced by the U.S. government's funding sources for most research, including educational research.

In educational research, the approach that has been historically regarded as the most important is research that focuses on the examination of how variables in a particular area of inquiry (e.g., reading achievement, motivation, teaching methods, intelligence) relate to each other. Numbers, inferential statistics, and generalizability of findings to a population are among the primary considerations in this view. The "highest" form of research is manipulating one variable (e.g., a teaching method), while holding all other variables steady or balanced (e.g., gender, socioeconomic status) and examining effects on an outcome (e.g., reading achievement) and comparing the effects on a treatment group as compared to a control group. This kind of experimental research is referred to as the "gold standard." This approach is parallel to work in areas like pharmaceutical research. Oftentimes, this research uses statistical analysis and is known as post-positivist research. Historically, these methods were known as quantitative.

There are other research scientists who embrace the variability in research approaches. They value the advantage that multiple approaches bring: We, as a field, have more ways of examining phenomena that are of general concern and interest. Many of these other approaches allow us to explore research questions that move beyond the "what works for whom" and "under what condition" questions that limit what we can study. Many of these other methods fall under what is typically called interpretive (sometimes called constructivist) and transformative research. Historically, these methods were called qualitative.

These approaches generally view context as dynamic and are concerned that attempts to control these dynamic qualities may misrepresent what is being studied. These approaches are often concerned with the oversimplification of complex constructs (e.g., gender, social class, reading ability) through the naming of variables and the subsequent measurement and scaling that typically take place in post-positive research. These approaches are generally cautious around the generalizability of any group studied directly to other groups or populations. Instead, researchers in this paradigm are concerned with the credibility, dependability, and transferability of their findings. In the transformative paradigm, the utility of the research becomes of the utmost importance in evaluating the research.

Interpretivist and transformative approaches tend to focus on uncovering the meanings made by the participants and not on inferences made by the research about what is being studied. Finally, these approaches generally—but with some significant exceptions—tend to avoid the notion of intervention or experimentation as distortive and, in some cases, hegemonic (ruling or dominant in political or social context) in nature.

Our purpose in this book is not to compare or resolve these conflicting stances toward research. As we pointed out in an earlier chapter, the dichotomy between quantitative and qualitative research is a false one. We tend to focus on what all of these approaches share as they relate to the scientific method: clear goals and purposes; stated connections to other research; methods that are systematic, are rigorous, and draw on accepted standards; gathering and analyzing empirical data; interpretation of findings through theoretical lenses; and claims for significance that document what this research work adds to, or contradicts in, the existing body of literature. Have no fear—we walk you through all these steps in the second part of this book.

Our point in this chapter is that practice-based research—the point of this book—doesn't fall neatly into either of the two approaches (e.g., quantitative vs. qualitative). Nor do we see practice-based research as falling into some gray area between the two that is labeled as mixed-methods research. Rather, we see practice-based research as drawing on the three frameworks that we've talked about in the previous chapters (action research, design-development research, and transformative research). In some cases, people might think about practice-based research as aligned with Mertens's (2015) description of "pragmatic research," but her development of this area is limited and confounded at times with a mixed-methods approach.

We are devoting a good deal of attention here to the naming of research approaches because these terms matter in research communities. Practice-based literacy research is an approach suited to those who strive to improve the teaching of literacy in local settings, with implications for changed classrooms, schools, communities, and ultimately our society. What we'll show you in this chapter (and the remainder of the book) is that the method you use as part of your practice-based research is not the most important item to consider. Rather, we'd encourage you to think about practice-based research in terms of the following:

Pause and Reflect

Where do you stand in the "research wars"? What similarities do you see between the research wars and the "reading wars"? How can we disrupt both through practice-based research?

- Practice-based research is directed toward the identification of principles that can guide the growth of teaching practices.

- Practice-based research is contextual and involves both problem-posing and problem-solving efforts in these contexts.

- Practice-based research is theoretical in its focus on the context and principles being explored.

- Practice-based research is empirical and relies on data collection and data analysis to support claims made.

- Practice-based research is action oriented, relying on the introduction of changes as the impetus for inquiry into principles of practice.

- Practice-based research is connected to previous research conducted into the same topic and intends to contribute to this literature.

- Practice-based research is considerate of space and place and therefore is cautious regarding the generalizability of findings to other contexts.

- Practice-based research is dependable, credible, and transferable.

- Practice-based research thrives in collaborative contexts where expertise and work are shared.

- Practice-based research thrives in the context of radical imagining, where practitioners are aware of the constraints they operate under and are willing to ask "what if" questions, not just look for counterstances (Anzaldúa, 2007).

- Practice-based research is humanizing in its exploration of relational experiences at the center of the work.

- Practice-based research can be used as a transformative tool to address the oppressive forces limiting educational progress and the goals of social justice and equity; it builds communities that work together for change.

- Practice-based research is never finished: There is always another iteration to explore, or a new set of questions to address.

In short, our practice-based teaching, as a result of our practice-based research, is integral to who we are and how we teach in the classroom. It is neither optional nor additive. As practice-based researchers, we believe we are in a state of "becoming" as we develop new skills and expand the communities in which we work. Practice-based research is the very air we breathe as teachers, teacher educators, and educational researchers. We are glad to be in this space with you as we move into a full description of what practice-based research means to us and how it has looked in our learning and research spaces.

The Cycle of Practice-Based Research

While we will present on each of the components of the practice-based research process in great detail in upcoming chapters, we offer here an introduction to each. We use the term cycle in much the same way as it is often used in describing the elements of the writing process. We acknowledge that the danger associated with presenting the components as separate from each other is that they may be perceived as linear and fixed. Our point in presenting them as a cycle, as is often done in action research, community-based research, and YPAR, is so they might be interpreted as recursive.

Entering into the Cycle: Finding a Focus

Maybe you are thinking, "I don't have anything to write about." We have all engaged with writers who initially struggle with finding something important for them to write about. We also know that writers who are supported through a process approach (Smith, 2019) quickly realize that they have a lot to write about and that the more difficult challenge is choosing a topic for the moment. Choosing your point of entry into your practice-based research project can be difficult (even overwhelming) at the start, but it is necessary. We suggest some questions in the following section to guide you in "landing" on an entry point into your practice-based research project. We will stress in these questions the options of working with something that is not working as well as you would hope, extending something that has been going well, or questioning some of the consensual reality (Anzaldúa, 2015) that surrounds you and the young people with whom you work. Think about the literacy practices in your classroom, your instructional practices, and those of your young people:

- What are the most exciting moments in your teaching day?

- What are some areas in literacy that your young people excel at? Struggle with?

- What do you worry about at the end the day? What "gnaws" at you?

- What changes have you made recently in your practices, and how are those going?

- What might you be doing in your practice that you have felt you could never do? Or are not "allowed" to do?

- What aspects of your practice might you revisit in order for the young people in your shared learning space to become the kinds of people *they* want to become?

- What aspects of your practice might you revisit in order to grow the radical imagination of those same young people?

Engaging in Research with Children and Youth

Oftentimes research in schools is taught as something we only do in science; it's often taught as something to do for the annual science fair. This one-off attempt at research sends a message to young people that research is only something we do when we experiment on (and inside) our natural worlds. It also sends a message that research is a linear process. It becomes imperative that we expand those notions so that young people see research as an extension of the daily inquiry that fills their lives in and outside of school. To that end, we might

- Encourage young people (and provide spaces for them) to engage in research in all of the disciplines and in research that transcends the disciplines (from an interdisciplinary perspective);

- Talk with them about the practice-based research you are doing, why you're doing it, and why it's important to you; and

- Create spaces where the research that comes out of your classroom is shared widely—with other young people at your school and with your community.

Consider using quick writes to journal your way through your responses to some of these questions. Did those questions generate other questions? If so, write them down somewhere! As in topic selection in a process approach to writing, quick writes can help surface interests. Which ones are of greatest interest? Here are some filters you might consider:

Start local. Don't think about changing the world of literacy instruction right away.

Think small. Maybe you don't work with the entire class right away, but with a small group, or if you have multiple sections (because you are departmentalized), you only start with one class.

Convoke your radical imagination. Don't let perceived boundaries, based on what you think you might be allowed to do, get in the way. Similarly, don't look for counterstances (Anzaldúa, 2007)—in fact, don't just think outside of the box, get out of the box.

Recruit your youth as collaborators in your research. Might YPAR serve as the centering for your practice-based research? What if the youth were engaged in their work (with you as a co-researcher) and they were engaged in your practice-based research (as co-researchers with you)?

Be mindful of resources. Accept the limits you have on resources to support your work and work within those confines.

Consider potential colleagues. Who else in your space might collaborate with you? Who might be a sounding board for your work? Who might support you in this endeavor?

Think in iterations. At its center, practice-based research is about iterations. How can you approach what you want to do in steps?

Be mindful of who benefits from your work. Ask follow-up questions: Who benefits from this work and how? What is being disrupted through this research?

One teacher, Amanda Rodriguez, found the focus of her practice-based research question as part of her growing desire to "turn more over to the children." In doing so, she discovered that her definition of leadership was different than that of her youth. She decided to follow that lead, and thus her practice-based research study was born.

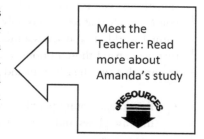

Meet the Teacher: Read more about Amanda's study

Stating Your Research Question

Some perfectly viable research questions that might be asked in empirical research include the following:

• Why do the young people in our classroom hate writing?

• How does reading in trade books motivate readers?

• Why do students choose informational texts that are too difficult for them to read?

These are all important questions that could very well come from a teacher thinking about practice in her classroom. *But*, these questions are not action oriented. Practice-based research is action oriented—that is, the research question that we ask, as practice-based researchers, leads to some action being taken and studied carefully through iterations.

An action-oriented plan is derived from what you will do to innovate in ways that attempt to address a challenge or an opportunity and to disrupt the commonplace. In practice-based research, our research question would lead us to plan an action to take. For example, here are some practice-based research questions that demand an action:

- How might increasing the amount of time for writing in a workshop shift students' attitudes about writing?

- How might providing opportunities for young people to talk about the books they are reading (those that they have selected) shift their motivation to read?

- How does removing the levels and level restrictions in our classroom library affect the choice of informational texts for independent reading?

These are the types of questions that beg for action on the part of the teacher, in response to the young people in her learning space. Furthermore, these questions do create spaces for disruptions in the traditional curriculum.

However, while these questions create spaces for disruptions in the commonplace, they are not quite transformative in nature yet, not in the way that Anzaldúa, Castoriadis, Freire, and others have talked about. Questions that are more clearly transformative might go something like this:

- How does providing culturally sustaining children's literature or young adult literature contribute to the growing identity of the young people in our learning space? And/Or (depending on the context), how does that same literature open, expand, and push back on long-held beliefs about people of color by young people from White backgrounds?

- How does increasing the amount of quality literature that explicitly reveals and confronts racism in society lead to activism on the part of my youth and me?

One preservice teacher, Sarah Viviano, re-framed her research question multiple times before she found just the right one. Most of her reframing was done as her observations in her classroom became more focused. This is very common, and we encourage you to follow Sarah's example for being open to writing, rewriting, and re-rewriting your research question.

We offer further support for asking your research question in Chapter 7.

Meet the Teacher: Read more about Sarah's study

Conducting a Literature Scan

You can count on the fact that there are others who are researching the area you are planning to study. Reading into the body of work that has been done before you (typically called "the literature") will sharpen your focus and give you access to tools and strategies that you can build on in your work. Don't let your reading in the literature discourage your focus. If there are others engaged in this area, this means that important work is going on that you can become part of. This stage of the process is perfect for pointing out the interactions between stages. Your reading in the literature may very well help you reshape the question you have framed. In Chapter 8, you will find greater details on this step as you begin to engage in your own research.

Initiate the Action Plan

This next step is at the heart and soul of practice-based research. It involves the "doing" part of your study. What steps will you take to enact your study? We are not asking you to think in terms of "fidelity to implementation" because that language belongs in a different paradigm. We are, however, asking you to think about how to be systematic about enacting what you do and how you do it. Several things you'll want to think about include the following.

Collecting data

The gist of data collection is to systematically gather data that will help you study your actions. You can collect a variety of data, including observational data, interview data, focus group data, and artifacts (including images and the work your children/youth produce). You might also consider audio or video taping your teaching. This step is explained more fully in Chapter 10.

Analyzing and Interpreting Data

This is perhaps one of our favorite parts of practice-based research, as this step allows us to "see" what is happening in the process. There are a multitude of analysis tools, and all are dependent on the research questions you asked, the theoretical frame(s) that guide your work, and the type of data you collected. We explain this component more in Chapter 10, too.

Iterating and Adapting

One of the important features of practice-based research is the flexibility you have in the design of your study. You may plan for phases in your study. You may, along the way, find it helpful to make modifications in your work that you may not have planned for initially. These turns are expected and once again point to the ways in which this cycle may shift back to a clarification of your question or a revision in your data collection tools or the features of your innovation. This is where we draw heavily from the design-development work explained in Chapter 4.

Reflecting and Sharing Your Results

This step involves taking two steps back and looking at the action research project from a "big idea" perspective. Many teachers think about their findings in terms of their research question—what you can tell others about your findings (see Chapter 11 for examples of disseminating your research). We would emphasize here the importance not just of "telling" or "reporting" but of actually making an argument for why your findings should be trusted and why your findings are new and important for others to consider in their own work. As

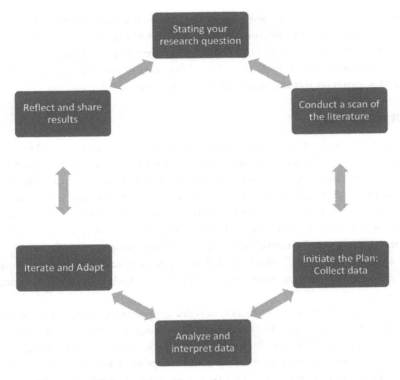

FIGURE 6.1 Cycle of Practice-Based Research

practice-based research becomes more transformative in focus, then the dissemination may go beyond just the sharing of results and into an actual activist agenda.

Many teachers think about how what they learned in their research project leads to their next practice-based research project: What do you still want to know about your practice? Where is the natural next step for you to take in terms of studying your own practice? One of the important things to remember is the cyclical nature of practice-based research. It is not linear. While we just presented the steps in a linear format for explanation purposes, practice-based research often operates from a recursive stance—thus the double-arrowed direction between the components in Figure 6.1. It is not uncommon to move back and forth between the steps as we solve problems of practice.

The Relationship Between Reflexivity and Practice-Based Research

We are advocates for teachers as reflective practitioners and realize the long-standing status reflection has had in our field. However, as we have written elsewhere (Sailors, 2019), critical reflection (or praxis) is different from reflection, as praxis exposes contradictions of our constructed realities, especially those that lead to injustices in our institutions (in this case, education). Praxis requires that we *do* something about those constructed realities once we expose the contradiction. And, while reflection can help teachers improve their practice, reflection alone may not be enough to move toward anti-hegemonic practices, since "reflection maintains an objective view of the world, one in which 'I'm not responsible for [X]' because 'I can only do so much'" (Sailors, 2019, p. 443). To that end, here we show the difference between reflection and reflexivity, in the hope that these differences might help you move toward a practice-based research project that is transformative in nature.

Reflection: In a Single Loop

Reflection allows us to look closely at our practice and ask questions like, "How can we do what we do better?" Reflection is the epitome of what it means to be a professional, where professional knowledge is valued. In fact, Schön (1983, 1987) described reflection to be as rigorous as the development of theory in scientific research. His notions of reflection are metacognitive in nature, involving both reflection-on-action as well as reflection-in-action. Argyris and Schön (1978) called this type of reflection single loop. Zeichner and Liston (1987) further developed Schön's notions of reflection through what they called "reflectivity," which included explicating and clarifying assumptions and underlying predispositions—and critical reflection, which incorporated moral and ethical criteria.

It was in keeping with notions of teachers as reflective practitioners that the work known as thoughtfully adaptive practice was developed. Harkening from the roots of research on explicit teaching of comprehension, this body of research on teacher education grew to study in-the-moment adaptations of literacy teachers and the professional development that supported them (Hoffman & Duffy, 2016). This line of work has focused on preservice teachers (Duffy et al., 2008) and in-service teachers (Vaughn & Parsons, 2013). The literature is clear on the need for teachers to have a vision for their classroom (Allen, Matthews, & Parsons, 2013) and to be adaptive in their teaching. According to the theory and research to support it, teachers become adaptive in their instruction and make instructional decisions for their students based on the selection and adaptation of ideas from a variety of ideologies, methods, materials, and programs (Hoffman & Duffy, 1999).

Reflexivity: In a Double Loop

While practices may change through reflection, we can only get at social change (i.e., addressing structures of inequities, power imbalances, and forms of oppression and exploitation in societies) through reflexivity. Castoriadis' metaphor of magma can support us in explaining how the institution of education (and its governing society) exerts power and pressure on teachers to teach certain curriculum and engage in traditional practices. Learning spaces do not operate in isolation of the community and society in which they exist. As such, learning spaces often embody social norms, values, and actions seen in the larger community.

Take, for example, the day before the 2016 election. Misty was sitting in a third-grade classroom (Sailors & Manning, 2020). The teacher was engaged in an interactive read aloud of *Separate Is Never Equal: Sylvia Mendez and Her Family's Fight for Desegregation* (Tonatiuh, 2014). The teacher was committed to supplementing the scripted curriculum her school handed her when she started teaching three years earlier. In fact, her practice-based research question oriented around disrupting the curriculum, placing the experiences of her third graders at the center of her work as a teacher, and using children's literature that directly addressed issues of race and racism. This read aloud was one of the many spaces she created as part of the iterations in her action plan.

At one point in the book, the teacher paused to engage the children in a conversation about why the secretary at the school invited the two light-skinned cousins to enroll but not the children with dark skin. In fact, the secretary told the children that "they must go to the Mexican school" (p. 8). Holding the book so the children could still see the image of the five children, the teacher invited the children to "turn and talk to your neighbor about what you're thinking right now." A buzz filled the air as the children eagerly began their conversations on the carpeted area of the room. That is, until one child sitting just at her feet turned to two girls next to him and said, "You go back to Mexico. And you go back to Mexico," pointing to each in turn. The classroom was a microcosm of our larger society—the language of the White child mirrored the political rhetoric of the day as he spoke to his Latinx peers.

While the teacher may have been in a space of reflection-in-action at that moment, there was something larger that was driving her practice—praxis. Praxis is the space where practice and action commingle and interact with each other. Argyris and Schön (1978) referred to this as double-loop reflection. That is, teachers are not only reflecting on their practices but are actively thinking about the structures that surround them (and their children/youth) that have created and maintained systems of oppression and exploitation. While some might view the statement of the White boy as uncomfortable and might just say something like, "Now, now. Everyone has the right to be here," this teacher saw this as an opportunity to disrupt notions of anti-immigrant sentiment that had crept into her classroom. Through intentional planning to rehumanize people who are immigrants via children's literature on immigration, she created spaces where she could disrupt grand narratives that were circulating from the highest political office in the United States. Her practice was grounded in praxis-oriented practices. That is, she was in a space of reflexivity.

Reflexivity allows us to decenter practice that we take for granted and ask questions related to *why* we do what we do. While reflection can be seen as objective and analytic, reflexivity demands that we are involved personally, morally, and ethically to question and dismantle systems of oppression that exist within our classrooms, schools, communities, and society. A reflective teacher might explore different ways to walk children in the hallways a bit more quietly. She might look at different ways to motivate children to be quiet. Or, she might do what the other teachers around her are doing (e.g., have all children walk with their hands behind backs or follow the line of tiles that parallel the halls because "we've always done it that way"). Or, she might come up with her own way of keeping the children quiet.

A reflexive teacher, on the other hand, would question the nature of *why* we make children walk quietly in the hallways, in a straight line, with their hands behind their backs (and sometimes with "bubbles" in their mouths). This teacher would find herself in a double-loop reflection: thinking about why we do

Pause and Reflect

What role does reflection play in your practice? What role does reflexivity play in your practice? What are some practices that you'd like to take a more reflexive stance on? How might a practice-based research project be a collaborator with you in moving more in the direction of reflexivity?

what we do with children. The praxis part of this pedagogy is to then *act* upon reflexivity. That same teacher might not only ask these kinds of questions, but she might also have a conversation with children about how they might accomplish their objectives (e.g., walking to music) while rejecting systems of oppression (e.g., walking with a "bubble" in their mouths). Yes, (especially) very young children can think about regulating their bodies in time and space without an "overseer" mandating their every move.

Collaboration and Cultures of Inquiry

We return to note the importance of practice-based research not only in taking action but in reshaping our own professional lives as practitioners who research. There is a broad consensus that participation in research, as part of professional development, can improve the quality of teaching through a focus on reflective processes. Zeichner (2003) reviewed a set of studies focused on this application of action research. He identified several conditions under which school-based teacher research can become a transformative professional development activity. He pointed to the importance of "creating a culture of inquiry that respects the voices of teachers and the knowledge they bring to the research experience (as) a key dimension of teacher research programs that are successful in enabling . . . teacher and student learning" (p. 318).

Mostly, in these studies, teachers were given total control over the critical decisions ranging from determining the focus for their research, to formulating questions, to selecting the methods to be used. Teacher appreciation for the challenges of conducting action research was common. Zeichner emphasized that listening to and studying their students carefully puts them in a place where they are willing to approach teaching from a more reflective standpoint and give their pupils more input into classroom affairs. Zeichner also pointed out the importance of collaboration over an extended period of time. This kind of collaborative work is useful in clarifying norms and standards within a community of practice for conducting quality work. Surprisingly, there was no clear evidence across these studies for the importance of preparing teachers in the processes of doing this kind of research.

While the impact on researchers is certainly an important aspect of action research, our position goes beyond this outcome to make the claim that this kind of research can contribute to theory in educational processes. We try to be careful in distinguishing between teacher inquiry, which is solely for the benefit of the teacher and in the immediate contexts, and practice-based research that, in addition, is working to inform theory. We would also point out that our use of the term transformative is a bit broader than the focus for Zeichner's review. Zeichner—and the studies considered in his review—tended to focus on the transformation of the teacher thinking and practices and not on the transformation of the institutions themselves. Our view of transformative research includes both. For further discussion of these issues, we recommend Schmuck (2009) as an insightful collection of articles that take a critical look at action research.

Our use of the term practice-based research is intended to take a clear stance that this kind of research is defined by what is being studied (practice) and not so much by who, on the inside of practice, is doing the study. Teacher research, in our experience, has been critiqued by those setting standards for what really counts as "just teacher research." We hope that in disrupting this and moving toward practice-based research we are refocusing on the practice and not just on who is doing the research. And, in grounding practice-based research in the transformative paradigm (as one of its roots), we hope to help teachers create spaces in their classrooms where they work with their youth for a better today and tomorrow and, ultimately, for our society as a "more human dwelling place" (Ginwright, 2008, p. 14).

Pause and Reflect

In his work, Ginwright (2008) talked about making our society a "more human dwelling place" (p. 14). What role do teachers play in making this vision a reality? What role can practice-based research play in supporting such a vision?

Summary

In closing this chapter, we return to our commitment to the importance of researchers using their radical imagination to guide change. Practice-based research is about exploring possibilities we might have never considered in the face of forces of constraint. Imagination must win out in this struggle. Transformative practices change in fundamental ways how we engage with our colleagues and possibly even our students as co-learners and activists. We will stress throughout the chapters that follow the close relationship between practice-based research and learning to teach. The examples we will draw on—better stated as "the inspirations that we draw on"—are informed by our work not just with in-service teachers but with preservice teachers as well. The commingling of research and teaching in practice is not an option or something to be delayed. We must begin at the beginning.

Points to (Re)Consider

Think in terms of your practice. What aspects of your practice might you want to critically study? What is the role of the young people in your classroom inside your practice-based research project? How does their role inform how you refer to them throughout your study?

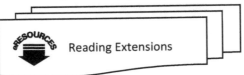

Reading Extensions

Children's Literature Cited

Tonatiuh, D. (2014). *Separate is never equal: Sylvia Mendez and her family's fight for desegregation.* New York, NY: Harry N. Abrams.

References

Allen, M. H., Matthews, C. E., & Parsons, S. A. (2013). A second-grade teacher's adaptive teaching during an integrated science-literacy unit. *Teaching and Teacher Education, 35,* 114–125. doi:10.1016/j.tate.2013.06.002

Anzaldúa, G. (2007). *Borderlands/La frontera* (3rd ed.). San Francisco, CA: Aunt Lute Books.

Anzaldúa, G. (2015). *Light in the dark: Luz en lo oscuro: Rewriting identity, spirituality, reality.* Durham, NC: Duke University Press.

Argyris, C., & Schön, D. (1978). *Organizational learning: A theory of action perspective.* Reading, MA: Addison Wesley.

Duffy, G. G., Miller, S. D., Kear, K. A., Parsons, S. A., Davis, S. G., & Williams, J. B. (2008). Teachers' instructional adaptations during literacy instruction. In Y. Kim (Ed.), *57th yearbook of the National Reading Conference* (pp. 160–171). Oak Creek, WI: National Reading Conference.

Ginwright, S. (2008). Collective radical imagination: Youth participatory action research and the art of emancipatory knowledge. In J. Cammarota & M. Fine (Eds.), *Revolutionizing education: Youth participatory action research in motion* (pp. 13–22). New York, NY: Routledge.

Hoffman, J. V., & Duffy, G. G. (1999). In pursuit of an illusion: The flawed search for a perfect method. *Reading Teacher, 53,* 10–16.

Hoffman, J. V., & Duffy, G. G. (2016). Does thoughtfully adaptive teaching actually exist? A challenge to teacher education. *Theory Into Practice, 55*(3), 172–179. https://doi.org/10.1080/0 0405841.2016.1173999

Mertens, D. M. (2015). *Research and evaluation in education and psychology* (4th ed.). Los Angeles, CA: Sage.

Sailors, M. (2019). Re-imagining teacher education. In D. E. Alvermann, N. J. Unrau, M. Sailors, & R. Ruddell (Eds.), *Theoretical models and processes of literacy* (7th ed., pp. 430–448). New York, NY: Routledge.

Sailors, M., & Manning, L. (2020). *Justice-oriented literacy coaching: Toward transformative practices.* New York, NY: Routledge Press.

Schmuck, R. A. (ed.). (2009). *Practical action research: A collection of articles.* Thousand Oak, CA: Corwin.

Schön, D. A. (1983). *The reflective practitioner: How professionals think in action.* New York, NY: Basic Books.

Schön, D. A. (1987). *Educating the reflective practitioner: Toward a new design for teaching and learning in the professions.* San Francisco, CA: Jossey-Bass.

Smith, A. (2019). Waves of theory building in writing and its development, and their implications for instruction, assessment, and curriculum. In D. E. Alvermann, N. J. Unrau, M. Sailors, & R. Ruddell (Eds.), *Theoretical models and processes of literacy* (7th ed., pp. 65–83). New York, NY: Routledge.

Vaughn, M., & Parsons, S. A. (2013). Adaptive teachers as innovators: Instructional adaptations opening spaces for enhanced literacy learning. *Language Arts, 91,* 81–93.

Zeichner, K. M. (2003). Teacher research as professional development for P-12 educators in the USA. *Educational Action Research, 11*(2), 301–326.

Zeichner, K. M., & Liston, D. (1987). Teaching student teachers to reflect. *Harvard Educational Review, 57*(1), 23–49.

Conducting Practice-Based Research

CHAPTER 7

Formulating Research Questions in Practice-Based Research

Preview: This chapter signals a shift in the book. In the previous section, we introduced you to the roots of practice-based research. In the chapters that fall under this second part of the book, we will walk through each of the elements of conducting practice-based research. We do not wish to suggest that the process of doing practice-based research is linear (and subsequently, simple). Everything about this type of research is cyclical, iterative, messy, and very complex. We will emphasize these qualities within each of the chapters. We will presume that you are in a context where you are beginning to engage in this kind of research. For example, in this chapter, we discuss the process of generating research questions that can be studied using a practice-based approach. We discuss aspects of generative research questions and provide examples of research questions asked by teachers with whom we have worked.

Imagine this conversation between a teacher, Sara Dominguez, and her literacy coach (LC) captured at the time Sara was constructing her practice-based research question.

LC: How are you feeling about your study?

Sara: Well. I'm still wavering on the research question. We've settled into our YPAR study and now I'm hoping to settle into my research question. You know, over the years I've tried my best to perfect my classroom management skills in an

> ### Points to Consider
>
> What aspects of your teaching might you begin to study that would put you in a place of reflexive practice? What role do your youth play in the research question(s) you ask?

effort to increase my instructional efficiency. I'm really wondering why I'm so stuck on the type of "management" system I have in my class. And, at what point do I move away from "classroom management" and into something that puts them in the driver's seat for making their own decisions? I was very aware of that when we were talking about moving their identification cards to something "bigger" than just petitioning the principal to "let" us wear name tags. I don't want them to just wear name tags . . . that's too much like the school-to-prison pipeline. I've really been wondering about my role in framing our classroom so that they think they need name tags. It's probably because I've been controlling them too much for too long and correcting them when they're doing it "wrong." I'm really curious about supporting them in making decisions for themselves while understanding that their decisions impact everyone in our classroom. It's like the individual decisions we make in society—yes, we have the right to make individual decisions, but all our decisions, eventually, impact everyone in our society.

LC: [*nodding*] Hmm. What aspects of your instruction might you need to examine in order for this to happen? What "what if's" can you ask that would move you and your youth toward that place that you want to be with them?

Sara: Hmm. You mean like, "What if I stopped trying to control their every move?" [*laughter from both*]

LC: Well, maybe it *is* about who has the power and authority.

Sara: Maybe. I've also noticed how rote our classroom routines seem to be and how I feel like I have to correct everything they do. I wonder what it would look like if my classroom ran on something more "human" than the classroom management system adopted by our school?

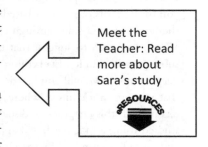
Meet the Teacher: Read more about Sara's study

LC: So, this sounds like the kind of question you could sink your teeth into *and* it would support your youth as they engage in their YPAR project. I can't wait to see how this plays out in your teaching!

Finding Your Question

Of all the features of practice-based research, the one feature that sets it apart from traditional research is the source of the research question. The question comes from within rather than from an outside source. In many ways, this makes perfect sense—not that we operate in dichotomies, but the opposite of *within* is *without*, and that is how traditional research is conducted: without a deep understanding of the context of spaces, places, and people who reside in classrooms, including the teacher and her youth. Based on our experience in asking our own practice-based research questions and working with teachers who are asking their own questions, many consider the *asking of the question* to be the most difficult. Finding our way into research questions can be as difficult as it is mind-opening. How does one come into and settle in on a research question?

Perhaps one answer can be found in Dewey's (1978) metaphor of "forks in the road" as moments for reflection that ultimately leads to praxis. These moments of reflection might become the source of initial research questions. We are aligned with what Schön called *problem solving* within a context. While this approach has some appeal, we frame the work of the practice-based researcher as problem posing. This Freirean notion of problem posing is part of a critical stance that resists starting with a problem that *others* may have framed and instead thinks critically around the challenges *we* are facing.

This leads to a broader question: Who gets to "name" the problem that research will address? Often, these are the people in positions of power and authority. As researchers, we recognize that framing our own research questions is at the center of agency in our work. So, we begin our consideration of research questions with a dialogue around various ways to pose the challenge (and frame questions) in the work we do with youth before we attempt to seek answers.

While we begin our exploration of practice-based research with a consideration of questions, this is not the starting place. Practice-based research questions always arise out of practice. Inchoate questions take

Pause and Reflect

Imagine hearing this at a faculty meeting: "We are having a problem with classroom management. Students are not on task. Students are not being held accountable for their work. What should we do? Maybe we need more rewards and clearer consequences to help solve this problem?"

- In what direction might these types of problem-solving statements take you? Who is directing the problem-solving statements? Are the questions directed toward critical change?

- What if the problem faced is one of a dull curriculum in which youth are resisting? How might the questions be reframed so that they are problem posing rather than problem solving?

shape in the context of practice. In moments where the articulation of research is difficult, returning into practice is often the place to find clarity. It's a process, and these questions take time.

The Changing Nature of Practice-Based Research Questions

One of the things that makes this process a bit gentler is that in practice-based research we can change our questions along the way. Indeed, we expect our research questions to become more refined as we engage in the cyclical process of practice-based research. In fact, we hardly believe that traditional research is so linear or so rigid that scientists hold true to the exact question that launched their research. More traditional forms of research may require staying closer to your question than practice-based research, but the heart and soul of practice-based research encourages you to adjust and make changes as you move into your work. This is not "cheating "or "bad science" as long as you document the changes you have made and what led you to these changes. The only violation would be to claim that the questions you ended with were the ones you started with—because that rarely happens.

The types of questions we ask improve the more we practice asking questions, just as with all the other considerations of being a teacher. In many ways, we consider our questions to have matured in the very way our literacy teaching matured: We became better at it as we learned to do it. Take, for example, the types of questions we asked readers when we first started teaching. Not knowing anything better, we tended to re-create the kinds of questions we were asked when we were in school as children. It was not until we interacted with some-one else (a more knowledgeable other) that we framed and reframed the kinds of questions we asked readers at the guided reading table. This is the same with asking research questions—ours became more carefully articulated and became closer to engaging us in praxis with our interactions with others. In our initial steps into research, we tended to replicate the kinds of questions that we saw researchers ask before: What is the best way to teach reading? If we teach phonics more explicitly, will we get better results? How can I raise my kids' test scores? These are not the questions that drive practice-based research, nor are they the kinds of ques-tions that grow out of the deep problem-posing work that researchers must do. Over time, our own research questions have matured as we have grown to appreciate and trust the questions *we* find interesting, that are aligned with *our* commitment to improving the human condition, and that the people with whom we engage in research want to study.

Asking Generative Questions

In many ways, writing a research question is about finding something that moves you from reflection (a first step) to reflexive practice (exposing contradictions inside socially con-structed realities). Some people talk about the qualities of "good" questions (Pine, 2009), but we like to think of questions in terms of how generative they are. First, a generative ques-tion is meaningful, compelling, and important to your life as a teacher and your professional growth. You have to love your question with a passion, and you have to want to use it as an engine for your research. No one else can find your question for you, but a good colleague (like the coach in the opening scenario) can facilitate a conversation with you in order to help you come into the question. A generative question is manageable within the context of your work. It is focused and not so big or ambitious that it requires enormous resources to answer.

Engaging in Research with Children and Youth

Asking generative questions of ourselves is very close to the kinds of questions we want our young people to ask during inquiry projects and youth participatory action research projects. To support young people in asking generative questions, we might,

- Engage them in a mind-mapping activity where they identify those areas of their life that are close to their heart;
- Engage them in dialogic interactions where you get to know them as individual people who live within a collective community; and
- Help them "land" on a question that centers their experiences.

Second, a generative research question should be important for your youth. Ideally, they would have a hand in helping you identify what you will study. But, if that is not the case, at least your question will stem from inquiry in which you all are engaged. For example, we saw Sara reframe her question in light of the YPAR project of her youth. That's a perfectly viable way to begin a question: What features of your teaching (think in terms of activity structures) do you need to question so that your youth can fully explore their research questions? For Sara, it was a matter of letting go of her control so her youth could grow into their understanding of how their world tries (at every turn) to control them. In many ways, she is teaching them to resist. At the very least, pursuing your research question should lead to benefits for your youth.

Third, a generative research question both invites and is spurred by action. Because of the cyclical nature of practice-based research, your research question should spur you to action—not just to "change" your practice (or to "improve" it), but drawing from the deep sense of urgency that drives your teaching. Teachers come into teaching for a variety of reasons, one of which is to improve the human condition. We do not mean this in a "great savior way" (e.g., "I want to make their lives better") but in the sense of "we need to take specific actions to right the injustices from our past and present selves." Through this lens, a generative question will grow out of that need to act and will become the impetus for that action.

Fourth, a generative research question is authentic. It is yours. You have to own it. You can seek support from your colleagues (peers, coaches, instructors) who can help you shape your question, but only you can *ask* your question. Take the formation of Iris Treinies' research question, for example. Iris worked through several questions with her literacy coach in her practice-based research study. She was well on her way to asking her question early in the study; she just needed to engage with her literacy coach in order to get to the question *she* wanted to ask. A well-meaning colleague (or coach) can make lots of suggestions for what you might study. But, in order for the study to be yours, you have to trust yourself in order to find your generative question. Revisit your "what if's" and try them out: Say them aloud and talk with other people about them. Talk to your young people in your classroom about them. Keep talking about your "what if's" until you settle in on one that you want to study.

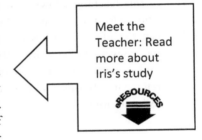

Meet the Teacher: Read more about Iris's study

Fifth, a generative research question will not have a *yes* or *no* answer. Questions like "Will this work if I do this?" may sound appealing and answerable (which they are). Often, teachers are tempted to look at one component of their activity structure and ask questions such as, "Will my young people become more motivated if I introduce more culturally relevant books into our read aloud?" The answer is "Yes." However, these *yes/no* questions do not lead to more questions, which is what generative research questions will do. The question Sara asked earlier ("I wonder what it would look like if my classroom ran on something more 'human' than the classroom management system our school has adopted?") is generative as it is going to lead her to more questions ("What will happen if we . . ." and "How can we . . . in order to . . .") that become inclusive of the young people in her classroom.

Sixth, and finally, given our focus on transformative practice-based research, we also believe generative questions draw on (capitalize on) our radical imagination. A generative question will challenge the assumptions and power structures that surround our practices and will create a space where we can envision a just tomorrow by thinking about and acting within a just today. We often encounter teachers who tell us they want to bring social movements into their classroom. The use of our radical imagination allows us to do that as it allows us to start with questioning our own assumptions (and the roots of those assumptions) as we fold our youth into those very practices with us.

Moving Toward Generative Questions

In many ways, we (as teachers) are in a constant state of improving what we do. Years ago, we were told if only we could move away from a focus on ourselves and tasks to a focus on our youth, all would be good in our classrooms and our young people would grow intellectually and otherwise. This is an important trajectory of a teacher's concern and focus and usually leads to reflection and reflective teaching. However, as we pointed out in earlier sections, this type of reflection is devoid of questions related to being anti-hegemonic in our teaching. From a critical practice perspective, being reflexive in our teaching allows us to move from reflection to a space where we can decodify structures of oppressive power and authority. We can find our way on this path (toward reflexivity) through asking generative questions.

Pause and Reflect

- Think back to those aspects of your activity structures that you identified in Chapter 2. Which of the components were you puzzling through? Were you asking questions related to any of them?

- Where those questions generative in nature?

- How can you reframe your questions so that they are generative?

Trying It Out

We now encourage you to "try on" the shawl of practice-based research through asking your own generative questions. This "trying on" process is an important part of moving in the direction of critical practice—you have to like how it "feels" on you. And, that "trying on" stage starts with your research question. Here are some recommendations to help you get started:

- Revisit the activity structures that you identified in Chapter 2. Ask a research question that pushes you toward reflecting on your teaching. What have you been puzzling over? What keeps you up at night? What aspects of your practice would you like to think more deeply about? Your first take on your question might start with "How can I . . ."

- Now, step away from that reflection question and explore the assumptions that surround that same activity structure. How is that activity structure limiting the possibilities of your teaching? Of the learning for your youth? Do those assumptions align with your goals and intentions for education and your time with your youth?

- Next, see if you can reframe your question into one that challenges those assumptions so that you can better serve your students and your vision for their future.

- Now, see if you can ask a "what if" question that would allow you to study your challenge to that assumption. Is it a generative question? Which of the aspects of generative questions does it address?

- Finally, as with trying on a physical shawl, turn to a colleague and "show" them your question. Get their input.

Pause and Reflect

Walk through the bullets we just presented and use them as a quick write. What insight do you have on the research paradigm that you might be operating based on how you are wording your question? Is that the paradigm that you want to operate in? If not, how might you reword your question to match your beliefs about knowledge and knowing?

Summary

As we conclude this chapter, we will encourage you to think in terms of "trying on as many shawls (research questions) as you like" until you find one that works for you. Generative questions are at the heart of practice-based research. The questions propel us into investigation and into an iterative cycle where we revisit and revise our guiding question(s). In finding your practice-based research questions, we encourage you to be patient. Asking and finding a practice-based research question is (in many ways) like investing in a nice shawl—you want it to

Points to (Re)Consider

Return to the opening questions. How has your thinking about your practice been affirmed? Shifted?

be worthy of your time and effort and to feel right on you. It has to be something you really want to examine and explore. At the risk of sounding redundant, we encourage you to talk with your colleagues about your question. It is through our interactions with others (and in saying our questions aloud) that we fully come to understand what we are trying to do (and say). Write your questions. Then rewrite them. Just as talking about our questions with others helps us frame and reframe them, so does writing them. Finally, we encourage you to talk with the youth in your classroom. They should be "in" this as much as you are.

Reading Extensions

References

Dewey, J. (1978). How we think. In J. A. Boydston (Ed.), *J. Dewey, how we think and selected essays, 1910–1911*. Carbondale, IL: Southern Illinois University Press. (Original work published 1910)

Pine, G. (2009). *Teacher action research*. Thousand Oaks, CA: Sage.

CHAPTER

8 Situating Your Research Alongside the Work of Others

Preview: In this chapter, we highlight the importance of connecting practice-based research with the work of other researchers who are exploring similar topics. Through engaging in what is called a literature review, we introduce you to the process of locating research studies and learning how to (re)present those studies as part of how you situate your work within broader, ongoing conversations about practice. This is a long and complex chapter. While you might want to skim through to get the gist, you definitely want to stop along the way and try out some of the things that we are suggesting related to your research focus.

In his book *Acts of Meaning*, Jerome Bruner (1990) described the very young child acquiring language as having been born into a conversation that is already underway. Talk is ubiquitous. The young child becomes a part of the conversation by watching, listening, joining in, experimenting with, and being mentored into the ways of making meaning with others by those who care for them. The child learns not only the forms of language but also the many functions of language that are on display in practice. Learning

> ### Points to Consider
>
> How does your practice-based research connect to other research? What research is similar to yours? How is yours unique?

anything new, as Lave and Wenger (1991) reminded us, is a community effort.

Taking up the practices of research is no exception. You must associate yourself with others who are engaged in producing research—not just those who "know" research, but those who are actively engaged in "doing" research. You will become part of the conversation through your own research and by the conversations you have with your colleagues and mentors. In many cases, mentors are real people you work with on a regular basis to hone your research strategies and skills. Those mentors can be found in physical spaces that surround you (your school, your graduate courses, professional conferences). In other cases, your mentors are authors of research studies that you have read or will read. You can engage in those conversations through what is known as a *literature review*. We walk you through the concept of a literature review in this chapter. While we do not intend for this chapter to read like a procedural text, we do offer you some tips on stepping into a literature review process.

What Is a Literature Review?

A literature review, or a careful reading (and noting) of the important findings related to your practice-based research project, is the most typical way to situate your work within what the research community calls a "body of literature." When you review the literature (studies that have been done before yours), you are, in essence, situating your work next to others'. This is an important part of the research process for several reasons. Knowing what has been done before us (as researchers) helps us "see" where and how our work fits with the work of others who share our interest in a particular topic. Additionally, a review of the literature helps a researcher trace the progression of a topic or practice— where did the practice or topic start, and where is it now? A traditional view of a review of the literature says that the review allows for a researcher to identify where the "gaps" are in the research and how their research study "fills" the gap. We agree with that, and we believe that a literature review might also help researchers identify places of passion for their research. Your research should be something that you are passionate about and want to spend time exploring. People who say your research must be "unique" and "different" and that it must address "something never before studied" are simply repeating a well-rehearsed myth about research. There are no educational researchers (of whom we are aware) that conduct research on a topic that "has never been studied before." And, to say that to people who are "new" at research is simply disingenuous.

In short, a review of the literature is both a process and a product. As a process, we think about engaging in a literature review as delving into a corpus of research studies, housed across texts (usually journals), that orient around a particular topic (or in our case, practice). Connecting your own research to the work of others is not an option; it is a necessity. Through this work of connecting, you may learn how others are approaching the topic in ways that are similar to or different from yours. You will find theories that others are drawing on in their work. You may discover research tools that will help you conduct your own research. You may locate outlets for sharing your own work. And, most important, you will probably reshape your research question along the way as a result of reading the literature in which you situate your study.

As a product, a literature review acts as both a summary and a synthesis of previous research on a topic. As part of your final report on your practice-based research project, a literature review (in some ways) serves as a backdrop for your readers, providing them with a full understanding of your practice, including major findings related to it, theories that inform it, and methods that have been used to study it in the past. In so many ways, a literature review conveys to the reader that you (a) know the literature and have an in-depth grasp of research related to your topic and (b) are contributing to that same body of research through your study. Your literature review (as a product) is part of establishing your credibility as a researcher. We will discuss the various ways to organize a literature review in a later section in this chapter.

Some Cautions as We Begin

You will likely not do a comprehensive review of all relevant research on your topic. You are more likely to do a selective review of work that is most directly related to your interests. There is no magic number here (e.g., find 10 studies). You need to set parameters, though, or you will exhaust yourself in connecting to the field.

You may encounter articles that make claims regarding your area of interest based on their own examination of the research literature. Your main interest is in connecting research studies. Use these sources to locate the original research that is being done. Look for the sponsor of these interpretations and explore potential biases in the interpretations.

You may also find published literature reviews on your topic. These can be particularly helpful in making sense of areas where there is a large body of research. Look to these for the general conclusions that are being drawn. Look to see if there are particular studies that seem particularly important or even seminal.

Earlier in this book, we referenced "Googling it" as a form of research that people do all the time. This is not the sense of research we are exploring in this book. However, Google and other search mechanisms are useful tools for examining the work of other researchers who share your interests and passions. The processes for engaging with the existing literature on your topic have become so much easier than in the past. While working in a physical library has its merits, most of what you need to do can be done online using your local or university library. In this chapter, we will guide you on a step-by-step approach to accessing research literature.

Pause and Reflect

To what research will you connect yours to? What body of literature will you explore? How will you begin this process? Revise it along the way? Document it? What role do conversations with your colleagues play in your process?

Literature Review as a Process

In this section, we focus on the act of a literature review as a process for engaging in and with previously published research on your practice. We focus on how to locate the literature and what to do with it once you find it.

Where Is This Corpus of Literature?

Most scientific communities use research journals as the basic mechanism for (a) communicating around important work and (b) holding researchers to standards for research that must be met before the work is published. Journals create editorial advisory review boards made up of prominent researchers. Typically, research journals are open to anyone who wishes to submit their work for review. As manuscripts are submitted by researchers to a journal, the editors send these out to members of their editorial board for review. Publication decisions are made based on these reviews. Journals are often sponsored by professional associations but not always.

There are several prominent journals in literacy research. You may search their websites for details on their history, their editorial boards, their focus, and their sponsorship. They include the following:

- *Reading Research Quarterly*
- *Research in the Teaching of English*
- *Journal of Literacy Research*
- *Literacy Research and Practice*
- *Reading and Writing Quarterly*
- *English Education*

There are journals that publish research related to literacy that may not be just focused on literacy. They include the following:

- *Elementary School Journal*
- *Action in Teacher Education*
- *Teaching and Teacher Education*

Finally, there are scholarly journals focused on literacy that are peer-reviewed that sometimes publish research reports, but tend to focus more on a consideration of practices and their connections to research. They include the following:

- *The Reading Teacher*
- *Language Arts*
- *Journal of Adult and Adolescent Literacy*

Journals carry different levels of status within scholarly communities. This status, in the past, was associated with reputation among scholars. Today, the status of a journal is sometimes considered by the citation rates of articles that appear in that journal. Essentially, the citation rates are calculated by the number of times other articles published in research journals reference an article published in this journal. Citation rates and journal rankings based on citation rates have been challenged, but still these are commonly used indicators of journal quality.

Searching for Research Studies

While it would be nice for research studies to be organized in journals like fruit in your favorite grocery store (all Granny Smith apples are located in this bin [journal], while all Jazz apples are located in this bin [journal]), research studies related to your practice-based study are often found across journals. To find them, you have to dig through the various bins (journals) and look for them. While there are a few journals that are published only online, the general tendency among journals is to publish a print version of the journal with online access available. But, how is one to go about searching the literal thousands of research articles published each year?

Thanks to advances in technology over the past two decades, research has become more accessible for everyone. There are numerous search engines that will allow you to search for studies published on particular topics, by particular authors, with particular populations, and using particular methodologies. If the search engines you have access to go through something like a library, you may have free access to the original publications for downloading purposes.

We will offer a short introduction here that you can use to begin the search for previously published research on your topic. For this introduction, we will rely on Google Scholar as a search engine. You can access Google Scholar on any browser. If you access it through your university, you will have access to the actual articles. If you do not have access to journals through a library subscription, oftentimes you can locate research articles on individual researchers' web pages and on repositories such as ResearchGate and Academia.edu.

So, how does one go about locating a set of research studies on a particular practice? Let's say, for purposes of illustration, that we are interested in research into promoting reading comprehension through read alouds at the elementary level. We access Google Scholar and enter "promoting reading comprehension through read alouds elementary" in the search box. We did limit our search to publications 10 years prior (2009+). Of course, when we start to limit the search (e.g., time frame for studies), we will receive different outputs. We left the browser (Safari, in our case) to sort the results by its default: relevance. In Figure 8.1 we see the beginning of the results.

You will notice that not all of the links that were part of the output are reports of research studies. A typical search on Google Scholar may bring up synthesis papers, policy documents, individual blogs, or web pages with ideas on how to teach comprehension. Your results may look slightly different based on your level of access to the references associated with Google Scholar. In our search, we located over 7,750 findings. The order of display can vary, but often you will find that the more highly cited articles appear first. If you want to consider all published articles (with no date range), you can unclick on the date ranges on the left-hand side. If you click on the title of the article, you will typically be taken to the journal or to the publisher and find a full reference and an abstract of the article.

Engaging in Research with Children and Youth

Sometimes we need to support children and youth in searching for existing literature on their topic of interest. Some prompts to get them thinking may include,

- In what sources might you find your information? How do you know those sources are credible and trustworthy? How has the author of that source (those sources) established their expertise?
- Are the keywords you are using broad enough so that you can "sweep" enough studies but "narrow" enough so you don't capture an overwhelming number of studies?
- Should you organize your results by relevance or date? Which best suits your needs?

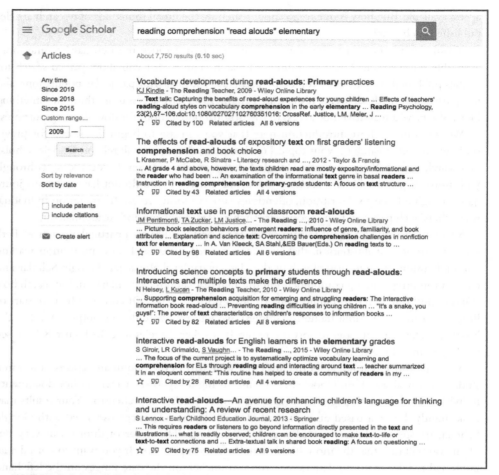

FIGURE 8.1 Output of Google Scholar Search

You will never follow and read these 7,750 links in your review. It is helpful to narrow your search to focus on your topic. One way to refine your search is to click on the icon next to Google Scholar on the top left of the page. Here you will find an advanced search option. This can be a useful tool in narrowing your findings. We would suggest that, for your research topic, you might want to look at some of the professional journals that are more general summaries of research in an area. For example, enter "*The Reading Teacher*" under "Return articles published in" and then click on the search icon. The results will include only those articles published in *The Reading Teacher* related to your initial topic. You may want to adjust the years being searched to be more inclusive of earlier publications.

Following the Breadcrumbs

Just to follow up on this example, in our search on read alouds in elementary classrooms, we came across a link to a study conducted by Kindle (2009) in *The Reading Teacher*. The study focused on the role of read alouds in vocabulary development. You will see that this is a research report: The authors looked carefully at the practices of four teachers and captured the benefits of read alouds with young children. While this article may fit our literature review search, it may not be exactly what we are looking for. Another strategy we use in broadening our findings is to "follow the crumbs." That is, we can look to see who else has cited this study. In Figure 8.1, you will see that this study has been cited 100 times (at the time we were writing this chapter). If you click on the "Cited by," you will be taken to a list of references of everyone who has cited the original article. If any of the studies that cited Kindle's study look interesting to you, you can go back to Google Scholar and enter the author and the title and locate that article.

Research Reviews

Most research reports give the reader a brief review of the research literature that is informing their work. This is the base the authors will use to make claims about the significance of the contribution. In your searching, you may also come across what is known as a "research review." These are articles that examine all of the research literature around a particular topic and synthesize the "what's known" in that area. They often go further to describe needed areas of research around questions that are still unsettled. These are useful because they have drawn together all studies (usually within a particular time frame) related to a specific topic. These are sometimes called *meta-studies*, *meta-analysis*, or *literature reviews*. For example, Jim (Hoffman et al., 2019) recently completed a literature review of the research on mentoring/tutoring in preservice teacher preparation programs. If that's your topic, then this research review can be a gold mine for you in locating the most recent research (at the time we wrote this chapter) on how mentoring/tutoring supports the learning of preservice teachers.

There are journals dedicated to publishing research reviews; the most prominent in education is the *Review of Educational Research*. If you access one of the issues online, you can see the various examples of topics included. In addition, other journals may publish research reviews as well. These research reviews are extremely important in keeping the field moving forward. Enter into your Google Scholar the term *research review* and then a topic (e.g., bilingual instruction), and the reviews in this area will appear in the results. Again, these can be very helpful. Look for the argument being made. What are the claims, evidence, and warrants?

What About Results That Are Not "Research Studies"?

When we describe an article as "not a research report," we do not wish to imply that an article that is not a report of research is unimportant. Many articles that are not reporting research are published in professional journals. These articles may be conceptual pieces (e.g., answering the question "What is transmediation?") or may offer syntheses around areas of inquiry. These articles may be very practice oriented and help us unpack practices and the support these practices have in research. Reading these kinds of reports can be very helpful in locating the research studies that are shaping the field. A research report states very clearly that the publication is reporting the findings from a study (with research questions, participants, methods, data, analytic methods, findings, etc.). Research reports are published just once. An author can write many articles around a topic and refer to research they have conducted, but the original research study is published just once. The exception to this rule can come in the context of a larger study when the researcher may report separately on different analyses that have been completed.

Organizing What You Find

As you locate articles that are of interest, you should begin to collect the links (if not the actual PDF files of these articles) in some way. We have seen this done in a variety of ways. In the (very) old days, people used to put each study they decided to keep on an index card. They would write the reference for the study on the card (using APA formatting; more on this later) and organize their cards based on some criteria that they were collecting (e.g., most salient findings, theoretical frames used, research methods used). They also would print their studies and keep them neatly organized in a binder. Today, we would be hard-pressed to find someone who still organizes their work this way.

Many people download PDF files and store them in a location on their computer or digital device. They use a word processor (e.g., Word, Pages, or simple text files) to keep a running list of the studies they are gathering. Still other people have moved into digital spaces that do all of this in one place, using what is called reference management software or applications. Some popular ones include Endnote®, Mendeley®, Zotero®, EasyBib®, and RefWorks®. These applications (some free, some not) normally consist of a database in which the PDF versions of studies are stored. They allow for bibliographic references to be entered, and they usually can be integrated with a word processor (e.g., Word or Pages) so that you can cite the research study as you are writing your literature review. They also allow for the generation of a reference list to be exported using the style format you choose (e.g., APA, Chicago, or MLA). Most of these applications also allow you to search references via online libraries, creating one less step in the search process for the end user. In some cases, you can "share" a project that you are working on with others, and groups of users can contribute to the building of a collection of studies.

Preparing a Bibliography

Finding studies to include in your literature review is the first step in the process of the review. And, while the search is time-consuming (especially if you are like us and start chasing the rabbit down holes that are not necessarily the holes you want to be in), creating a bibliography can both help keep you focused and support you in writing a synthesis of the literature in your next step (the review as a product). A simple bibliography is one in which you list the references that have informed your study. An annotated bibliography may be more appropriate if you are considering disseminating (sharing) your research with others (more on this in Chapter 11). The purpose of an annotated bibliography is to succinctly document the key points from a study (usually no more than 150 words) and to critically evaluate the study. Some people like to list the

Pause and Reflect

What resources do you have that will help you locate and organize research? Does your school or university have a subscription to one of the applications mentioned earlier? If not, what application do you have that will help you organize your information?

following in their annotated bibliographies: (a) purpose of the study, (b) research questions, (c) context of the study (demographics of the participants), (d) theoretical frame, (e) research methods, (f) findings, (g) implications, (h) limitations, and (i) how the study fits within the work. The annotated bibliography (in many ways) acts as a place where you can summarize those aspects of individual research studies that you gathered in the earliest parts of the process.

How to Read a Research Report

No doubt, you will encounter reports that are extremely difficult for you to access meaning. Research is filled with terminology and methods that become overwhelming. This may be particularly the case in quantitative research reports. At this stage, you are not trying to judge the quality of the research (you can trust that the journal editors have done this work for you); rather, you are looking for relevance to your research question and the significance of the work in informing your thinking. You will need to adjust your reading strategies to deal with the mass of information. You simply can't read every article from start to finish. You need filtering mechanisms. We have a few suggestions to guide you.

Think of every article you engage with as containing an argument for something. The researchers are trying to convince the reader (and the field) with their data that they have found something (this is their claim) that is important and new for the field to pay attention to. The "something" is the answer to the research question. The evidence is in the data they collected and analyzed. The "new" and "important" are relative to the review of literature they provide in the article. This is what you are reading for: the purpose, the claims, the evidence, the warrants that link the data to the claims, and the contribution—what's new? Beware of, or at least pay attention to, elements of persuasion the author might be introducing that are independent of the argument (e.g., the use of hyperbole, an appeal to the audience through the use of the word *we*, the pretense of certainty). Argument and persuasion are related but different.

It's really this simple at the start:

- Read the title carefully. The researchers are using the title to put the key terms in the most searchable place of all. All researchers want their work to be read and cited. The title is the invitation to read more.

- Read the abstract. The key elements of the argument should be present here. The abstract should tell you if this is an article that you want to spend time with in relation to your question.

- Read the introduction. Where do the authors situate their work? In what problem space? Read at least up to the statement of the research question. Is it still of interest to you?

- Read the conclusion. This will tell you what they found that they think is important to the field.

This first reading should help you decide if this is a report you want to invest further time into. If yes, then proceed:

- Look at the theoretical frame (this might be difficult to locate in some studies). Essentially you are looking for the general approach and assumptions about teaching, learning, students, and research that the researchers are using to guide their work.

- Look at the background literature reviewed. This will not only give you some insight into how research reviews are incorporated into an article; it will also give you leads on additional studies that you want to read.

- Look at the evidence gathered, the tools used, and the analytic methods. You might find things useful here in planning for your own study.

- Go to the citations for this article on Google Scholar and look at others who have referenced this study. Here again you might locate studies that are of interest.

Throughout this process, make notes on the PDF or in your research notebook. And, move the article into your collection of articles.

Literature Review to Situate Your Study

In this section, we focus on the act of a literature review as a product for contextualizing your practice-based research project. We focus on how to (re)present the literature you reviewed in ways that will support your reader in your final research report.

Organizing the Literature Review for Your Reader: Summarizing

There are several ways to present the information you gathered in your review of the literature for your reader. Some people approach the presentation of their review from a chronological perspective—that is, they summarize the studies (individually) and share them with the reader chronologically. Chronological representation is ideal when you are examining a practice that is represented widely in the corpus of literature and has had trends over time. One example of this might be approaches to small reading groups. You could present the ways small reading groups have developed in the literature over time, starting with what used to be called *small-group instruction* (read: round robin reading groups) and moving to the next stage, commonly called *guided reading*. While this is acceptable, it is not the most expedient way to demonstrate your understanding of the literature. In fact, this approach takes up a lot of space and does not allow for you to share the "big ideas" of the corpus of research with your reader.

Organizing the Literature Review for Your Reader: Synthesizing

A more concise way to organize your review of the literature is to synthesize across the studies that you gathered. You can think about (re)presenting the big ideas that transcend the research on your practice or topic. Synthesizing is the interweaving of key points from your summaries; most people present the information thematically. Thematic reviews of literature are organized around issues or key findings (although time periods may still play a role, depending on the subject). For example, from a thematic perspective, your literature on guided reading might be organized around the conditions under which guided reading is most effective (e.g., when teachers use flexible grouping), the role it plays in the language and literacy development of children who are learning English as an additional language, and the instructional moves teachers can make to support comprehension instruction in a small reading group. The big ideas you present are dependent on both what the literature says about your practice and what your focus is within that practice. The research on practices that are widely studied (such as guided reading, writing workshop, and read aloud) may be large enough that you'll have too much information to synthesize. Our advice is to stick with what's most important to your study and only report that.

As we pointed out in Chapter 1, the dichotomy of quantitative versus qualitative research methods is a false one. Our categorization of research closely follows the work of Donna Mertens (2014), who wrote about the "paradigms" of educational research. She named four: post-positivist, interpretivist, pragmatic, and transformative.

The reason we invoke the work of Mertens is that it offers us a way to think about synthesizing research, grounded in paradigms. Rather than thinking in terms of "this study used quantitative methods and this study used qualitative methods," we challenge you to think in terms of what the purposes of the research were, what the orientation of the researcher was, and how that orientation may have informed the findings. Thinking across research paradigms frees us to easily think across findings, regardless of how the data in our collection of studies was documented and analyzed using statistical, constructivist, pragmatic, or transformative research tools.

For example, in a research review on literacy coaching, Misty and her colleagues (Sailors, Minton, & Villarreal, 2016) located and synthesized across 118 studies. There were a variety of research methods employed across these studies. Because of this, Misty and her colleagues borrowed from Bair and Haworth's (2005) method for data analysis to synthesize across these studies. We first created a matrix that demographically documented important information from the articles (see Figure 8.2). Most of this came from the bibliography we created, as described earlier in this chapter.

Reference	Purpose of the study	Context of the study (e.g., grade level, ages of participants)	Theoretical Frame	Research Methods	Findings	How do these findings compare/challenge findings from other studies?

FIGURE 8.2 Example Matrix of Article Information

In addition, we inserted one more column and labeled it, "How do these findings compare/challenge findings from other studies?" This column allowed us to move into a space of synthesis with our research findings and see how the individual findings (for each discrete study) were related to each other. It was through this process that we juxtaposed, cross-compared, and integrated the findings from these studies, creating our emergent themes.

We're not suggesting that your methods for synthesizing across the studies you found be as extensive as what Misty and her colleagues did, but you might think about that last column as being the one that supports you in "seeing" the big picture across the findings. This column might be followed by a semantic map that helps you identify the themes that are represented within your literature review. For example, when we completed our synthesis of coaching studies, we found there were several "buckets" that we could use to talk about literacy coaching. You might think about the themes that are emerging from your collection of studies as buckets, or ways to talk about what the big ideas are that your synthesis is generating.

Writing the Review: Writing Like a Reader

In this section, we presume you are opting to present your literature review using a synthesis approach. We would encourage you to keep the following in mind as you present your findings to your reader.

- Be explicit about your criteria and processes for searching and analyzing studies. You can set your own parameters for your research review. You have latitude here. For example, you might limit your search to research published in refereed journals, to research studies published in the last 10 years, or to research that is focused on working with children living in economically disadvantaged communities. Very few studies based their literature review on all studies published on a topic. As a general rule, the broader the net the better. At a minimum, though, you must be explicit about the criteria for selection you used and why.

- Organize your report of the literature around findings. For example, in our coaching study, we presented our information based on (a) the evidence for the effectiveness of literacy coaching (on teacher practice and literacy achievement of children/youth in teachers' classrooms); (b) actions of coaches; (c) characteristics, experiences, and education of the coaches; (d) ways in which youth, teachers, classrooms, schools, and communities influence the way literacy coaching is enacted; and (e) coaching specifically related to comprehension instruction. Those "buckets" now become helpful to you in presenting the big ideas to your reader.

- Think in terms of important trends across studies in your collection and use those trends to organize your review. In many ways, the buckets (from the previous point) may help you think about these trends in the research that you'll want to share with your reader. You might choose to use those buckets as the organizational structure for your review. We used each of the items mentioned earlier (a–e) as the organizing structure for our literature review on coaching. As you transition from section to section, think about how you are presenting the buckets to the reader—are you relating them to each other? Creating a logical path for your reader to follow across the buckets? Remember, it is our job as writers to support our readers in making sense of the information we are presenting to them.

- Be on the lookout, too, for areas in the findings that you are not seeing, especially those that surprise you. This might be the last section of your literature review. Many people use these "holes" in the literature to demonstrate the need for their study. In other words, your review should show your reader where your study fits into the literature and how it extends the literature on your topic.

- Write concisely. While the literature review is important, it is not the heart and soul of your report—your methods and findings sections are. In your literature review, you want to present the big ideas to readers in a way that is to-the-point. Tell them just what they need to know so they trust your review. Focus on the synthesis, rather than the details of the study. For example, in our coaching study, it was much more important to talk about the mixed findings related to the effectiveness of literacy coaching than to talk about the many different sets of participants in each of the studies we reviewed. We saw it as our obligation to tell the reader that there were some studies that found coaching to be effective (and then we cited them), while others found it to not have any effects on teaching practices (and then we cited them). We felt that interested readers who wanted to follow up on the studies we cited could do so (and read more about the details of the various studies we read and reported on).

- You'll use evidence from your sources to substantiate your claims (related to the big ideas that you are presenting). While you can use quotes from studies, you want to use them sparingly. In fact, there is no reason to quote a finding if you can paraphrase it. However, you will want to be careful as there is a fine line between paraphrasing a source and plagiarism—always provide citations.

In summary, your synthesis of the literature should demonstrate to the reader that you have done your due diligence in situating your work next to the work that has gone before you. It should also demonstrate how your study extends the research on your topic. And, it should be well written.

Refining Your Research Questions

No doubt, as you read deeper into your area of interest, you will discover the work of others who are on a similar path of inquiry. You may find that the sources you read will help you focus your questions a little more tightly. If you are pursuing a design-development path, you may find ideas that are helpful in refining your plans for intervening. It is perfectly fine to build on and extend the work of others in research. In fact, this is an expected path for scientific inquiry. On the other hand, don't feel constrained to joining the group and following the path that is there. Use your radical imagination to pursue paths that have not been taken. Think locally, of the issues that spawned your interest, and design your own work that will become a significant contribution to the field.

Mentor Texts

Just as we tell our children/youth, find a text (or two) that might serve as a mentor text to you, specifically related to the way the author(s) present their literature review section. These mentor texts may be particularly powerful, clearly written, well argued, and significant. These may be reports of studies that were not directly related to your topic but were still notable. Having a few of these types of articles available as mentor texts for your own writing will be very helpful moving forward in your study and in your career. Additionally, as you move to the next chapter (where you'll design your study), you might also want to identify one (or more) mentor texts that can serve as your model for the design of your study.

Summary

We finish this chapter by encouraging you to stand alongside others who are exploring the same topic as you. In many cases, you'll see your practice-based research has the potential to inform a well-established field of research. In other cases, your work stands to inform a newer field. Regardless, your literature review will give you credibility ("I know the research on this topic—let me show you") and will help you show how your work not only aligns with a body of research but

Points to (Re)Consider

How is the act of writing a literature review informing your identity as an educational researcher?

extends that body as well. And, that is the purpose for doing educational research—to contribute to a body of knowledge larger than any individual or single classroom.

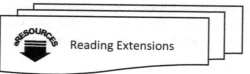

eRESOURCES   Reading Extensions

References

Bair, C. R., & Haworth, J. G. (2005). Doctoral student attrition and persistence: A meta-synthesis of research. In J. C. Smart (Ed.), *Higher education: Handbook of theory and research* (Vol. 19, pp. 481–534). Dordrecht, the Netherlands: Springer.

Bruner, J. (1990). *Acts of meaning*. Boston, MA: Harvard University Press.

Hoffman, J. V., Svrcek, N., Lammert, C., Daly-Lesch, A., Steinitz, E., Greeter, E., & DeJulio, S. (2019). A research review of literacy tutoring and mentoring in initial teacher preparation: Toward practices that can transform teaching. *Journal of Literacy Research, 51*(2), 233–251.

Kindle, K. J. (2009). Vocabulary development during read alouds: Primary practices. *The Reading Teacher, 63*(3), 202–211.

Lave, J., & Wenger, E. (1991). *Situated learning: Legitimate peripheral participation*. Cambridge: Cambridge University Press.

Mertens, D. M. (2014). *Research and evaluation in education and psychology* (4th ed.). New York, NY: Sage.

Sailors, M., Minton, S., & Villarreal, L. (2016). Literacy coaching and comprehension instruction. In S. Israel (Ed.), *Handbook of research on comprehension instruction* (pp. 601–625). New York, NY: Routledge.

9

Designing Your Study

Preview: In this chapter, we walk you through designing your practice-based research study. We highlight the most salient things you'll think about. The design for your study begins with the research question(s) you identified in Chapter 7. You might use a mentor text (or two) that you located in your review of the literature (that we described in Chapter 8). Our conversation about data collection and analysis will continue into Chapter 10.

Think about the decisions you make when you are preparing for a set of friends to come to your house. You ask yourself a host of questions as you are preparing. There are overarching questions that set everything in motion: What theme will I use? What decorations will I use to convey the theme to my guests? What food will I serve? And then there are logistical questions to ask: When is the best day? How many people will I invite? When should I send out invitations?

Although a bit trite to compare planning a research study to inviting friends over to dinner, planning a research study also comes with a series of questions

Points to Consider

What decisions will you make as you design your study? What standards and traditions will you draw upon for your study?

researchers ask themselves as they plan a study. Often, this planning is called *designing* a study. In this chapter, we will guide you through the process of designing your practice-based research study. In some sections, you will see reference to areas of a study we covered in earlier sections of the book. In other sections, you will encounter new information. Throughout, we'll ask you to make decisions about your study but to remain flexible, as often (because of its nature) educational research is tweaked as the study is enacted.

Introduction to Design

People might ask you about the design of your study: What is your research question? What methods are you using? Who are your participants? What data are you collecting? How will you analyze that data? These are starting points for what we call *research design*. Thinking about your design from the very beginning of a study is useful not only in thinking through a study but also in helping you explicate your study as you talk with your colleagues about it. This is not to say that the actual study won't change as it is underway, but the initial plan for the study is extremely useful as a framework.

In some cases, a research design may take the form of a research proposal. Master's students and doctoral students typically compose a proposal that describes the design of the study they intend to conduct as part of their program. The proposal is reviewed by mentors and advisors who then advise the student on ways in which the proposal might be strengthened before the data collection actually begins. In other cases, researchers might prepare a proposal to be submitted for funding. In both cases, the format for the proposed study may have quite explicit guidance on structure and organization.

If you are a researcher who is not planning a study as part of a formal degree (or program), you will still want to have a proposed design in place for several reasons. First, you may want to take the proposal to your professional learning network and ask for their feedback on it. Often, our colleagues can give us insights into our proposals that help us think about them in new and creative ways. Thinking through and documenting your design might provide you with talking points for conversations with colleagues.

Second, a proposal might come in handy when presenting your study to an administrator, which is often the case for teachers who want to engage in practice-based research. With or without an institutional review board (IRB) committee (those who approve research studies, following federal guidelines), you may be required to get approval from your campus or district administrators to engage in research as part of your practice.

Third, a proposal will help you plan and be prepared for your study. While the study will not be "set in stone" with its appearance on paper (as a design), it will at least be documented and, thus, a place for you to turn back to and revise as necessary.

For those of you who are using this book as part of required coursework, we make suggestions for components of study design, but ours is not the only way to approach design. We recommend you seek guidance from those who are mentoring and advising you through your program as you seek to align your design with the expectations for your program.

Some of what will be included in the design of your proposal has already been introduced in the previous chapters. This included identifying your research questions and aligning your work with that of others who have gone before you (via a literature review). Both of those become important in designing your study. Your research question should serve as the guide for what data you will collect and how you will analyze it. After all, what good will data do you if it does not help you answer your question?

Similarly, your review of the literature may have yielded some insight into how others approached research questions or topics similar to yours. You can think about their design as a mentor text for your study. For example, in the research synthesis we presented in Chapter 8 (Sailors, Minton, & Villarreal, 2016), we borrowed heavily from the works of colleagues who study doctoral student attrition and persistence (Bair, 1999; Bair & Haworth, 2005). It was their work that introduced us to a method for "handling" findings from other studies that were both post-positivistic and interpretivist. Although their work was very different from ours, their method provided us with a procedure that we could use with our data. And, thus, they were mentor texts for us.

Engaging in Research with Children and Youth

It is not uncommon to hear educators talk about starting with "standards" (local, state, and/ or national) and then supporting young people in aligning their interest with the standard. We are of the opposite belief—we believe that we can align any standard to the interest of a young person, especially when it comes to youth research that centers on their community and lives. We do this by,

- Engaging young people in conversations that support them in identifying topics of interest that are important to them;
- Dialogically listening (Helin, 2013) to them as to support them in learning the academic skills and strategies (Ladson-Billings, 1995) they need to take up in order to complete their research study and grow as scholars.

Designing a study in many ways is not just planning a study, it's also about making decisions. As you enter into your study, some things you'll need to consider (and make decisions about) include (a) the general method you will use, (b) who your participants will be and what role they will play in your research, (c) the data you will collect, and (d) the approach you will use to analyze your data. We address each of these, in turn, in this chapter.

Throughout each of these considerations, you may want to turn back to your community that surrounds you in this process (including mentors and advisors you might have and other teachers who are also engaged in practice-based research) as their insight into your decisions can be significant. Additionally, you'll want to consider the standards and traditions that you'll draw upon throughout the process. For example, if you decide to use post-positivistic methods (collecting scores as part of an outcome measure you want to use, for example), there is a long history and a standard set of expectations you will follow in doing so. Because of space limitations, we cannot list all the standards for each of the methods we describe in the sections that follow. We do, however, provide you with an overview of each.

Beginning With an Approach

Typically, research studies locate themselves within an approach that is linked to a set of assumptions, a set of tools, and some shared standards for what counts as quality. Many researchers tend to operate within a particular approach as they share in the values and perspectives represented in that approach. Other researchers might take up different approaches as a function of the kinds of research questions they hope to address. For example, if I am interested in comparing the effects of two different approaches to supporting fluency for first-grade students, then I would likely adopt a post-positivist approach that adopts experimental design features, uses assessment tools to measure outcomes, and applies statistical analyses that can become the basis for inferring toward a larger population.

If I am interested in how students' identities as readers and writers are shaped in particular contexts, then I would more likely adopt an interpretivist approach. The interpretivist (sometimes called constructivist) approach to research is largely driven by goals of discovering the underlying mechanisms or reasons for something happening or working the way it does, understanding people's lived experiences within a given context, or making sense of a particular phenomenon in education. Interpretivist approaches are commonly used to capture individuals' thoughts, feelings, or interpretations of meanings and processes (e.g., in an ethnography or case study) in an attempt to represent the views and understandings of the participants. Many of the studies that would ask questions such as these might be driven by analytic methods such as narrative methods, case study, grounded theory, phenomenology, and ethnography, to name a few.

Still other researchers, oriented toward activism, might take up a more transformative approach with such questions as, "Can I disrupt the sorting and classification of students based on ability by removing text-leveling practices in reading instruction?" The transformative approach to research is largely driven by goals of identifying and dismantling structures (cultural, political, historical, economic, and educational) within society that oppress people who are minoritized by their race/ethnicity, people who are working class, people with disabilities, people who are LGBTQ, indigenous populations, and girls and women. Researchers in this paradigm operate from the assumption that the world is an unjust place for many people, and the suffering of people can be traced back to colonization (and neocolonialization). Researchers who operate from this approach are committed to disrupting the deeply rooted tensions, contradictions, power imbalances, and forms of oppression and exploitation in our society.

In the case of your work in this book, you have already taken the first

Pause and Reflect

Are you leaning toward one of the approaches for your practice-based research study? Why? What (if anything) do you need to change about your research question so that it is aligned with the research approach you're leaning toward?

steps in identifying your approach as practice-based. Your philosophy is rooted in a pragmatic view that is locally situated and action oriented. You will draw on tools and traditions from other approaches as they suit your research questions that are practice oriented. For example, a researcher interested in promoting translanguaging in a multilingual setting might use interviews, discourse analysis, critical discourse analysis, observations, or informal measures to assess the effects of an innovation that has been introduced.

Generalizability and Validity

Regardless of the approach taken, a research study is always constructed as an argument around some claim that is being made or explored. In some cases this claim, in particular in practice-based research that draws on a post-positivist framework, is stated as a hypothesis to be tested. For example, the idea that adding student choice to book club reading will increase student motivation and comprehension takes the form of a hypothesis. In a practice-based study drawing more on an interpretivist set of assumptions, the claim may begin with a focusing question. For example, what happens when student choice is introduced into book club reading? Across these approaches, a research study still rests on a claim that is stated explicitly in the findings. The validity of the claims made rests on the evidence gathered and the warrants made in support of the argument. Researchers refer to this as the internal validity of a study. Is there a strong, believable case made for the claim that stands up to the logical scrutiny of the broader research community?

Using the example of increasing choice in book selection, a researcher might find that the increase in book choice leads to higher motivation to read as measured by a motivation assessment inventory (administered at the start and end of the study) as well as an analysis of log entries of time spent reading (from a baseline to the end of the study). But, what if the researcher wanted to claim that the increase in book choice leads to higher reading achievement? Without measures of reading achievement, this would not be a valid claim. The researcher might suggest that based on the established relationship in the literature between motivation and achievement, the findings from this study suggest a possible impact on achievement, but this is not a claim that is warranted by the study design.

A flaw in a study design can lead to an invalid claim (as in the case just described where there were no measures of achievement). The strength of an argument in support of internal validity is not as easy to determine. Again, in the previous example, the argument is strengthened by having multiple, independent measures of the outcomes in focus. This is something we will discuss again in the next chapter around the concept of triangulation.

External validity refers to the strength of the claim the researcher can make beyond the findings from the participants in the study. Can you make claims from your study of book choice that all students would engage similarly to the youth in your study? This concept of external validity is associated with the concept of generalizability. Who or what can you generalize to form your particular study? This is a major point of difference between most post-positivist research and interpretivist or transformative approaches. In post-positivist research, there is often the goal of inferring from a single study toward a larger population. In this tradition, the addition of control groups and attention to probability sampling become extremely important to making claims beyond any one particular study. In interpretivist and transformative approaches, context matters so much that there is typically no attempt to generalize beyond the group in the study. This is not to say that researchers using these approaches are not interested in documenting broad principles of understanding, but that they tend to rely on connecting across studies that others are doing or they engage in studies that gather more compelling evidence than the statistical inferences used in post-positivist research.

In a practice-based approach, we tend toward understanding generalizability as something that needs to be examined across multiple studies rather than within a single study. A practice-based researcher is more interested in the internal validity of a study and not the generalizability. This does not mean that a practice-based study might not rely on a comparison group of students in the design of a study: A researcher could start the introduction of choice with one book club group and then expand to a second and a third over time. Trading change across these different groups can strengthen the internal validity and the strength of the claim. Comparison groups are not always about generalizability.

Identifying Your Participants and Co-Researchers

Another consideration you will need to think about is who will be the participants in your study. There are several ways to think about this. First, you'll want to keep the traditions and standards related to your research approach in mind. Selecting participants under a post-positivist study is very different from selecting participants in an interpretivist or transformative study. In post-positivist research, what is important when selecting participants is that you do it randomly in order to remove the potential influence of external variables and to ensure generalizability of findings. In interpretivist and transformative research, participants are selected purposefully in order to best inform the research questions and enhance the researcher's understanding of the phenomenon being studied. Sometimes, we use *convenience* sampling (in interpretivist research), looking to those closest to us (physically and relationally) as participants in a study. Other times (especially in transformative research), we select those who will inform our shared research questions based on many factors, most of which include grassroots planning with people.

You'll also want to consider how many participants you need. In post-positivist research, this is referred to as a *sample size* and requires a statistical calculation before the study begins to ensure sufficient power. This is necessary to verify that the outcome of a study can be attributed to whatever is being studied (most often, an intervention). In interpretivist and transformative research, however, the number of participants in a study is dependent on fully informing the elements of the study. That is, researchers often continue to seek out additional participants until they reach what is called *data saturation*, which is when your data sources (interviews, focus groups; see the "Data Sources" section to follow) introduce no new concepts to you. We like to think of this using a sponge as a metaphor: When a sponge can hold no new water, it is saturated. The same goes for data collection: When you do not hear any new (or novel) concepts from your participants, you know you have reached data saturation.

Finally, if you're operating in the transformative research approach, you'll want to consider who your co-researchers might be. In most cases, they will be the children/youth in your classroom. After all, they are the ones with the most at stake in your research. In fact, in the "Meet a Teacher" resource online, you'll see how Amanda White was very open with her youth about the research she was conducting in their eighth-grade classroom. She and the youth made decisions about the study together; five of her youth became co-researchers with her.

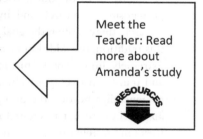

Meet the Teacher: Read more about Amanda's study

Once you've identified who your participants and co-researchers will be, you'll want to think about how to approach them and invite them to participate with you in your study. This is commonly called *recruitment* for most IRBs. There are several ways to go about this, but you'll want to keep in mind your research approach.

Recruiting for Practice-Based Research That Draws on Post-Positivist Assumptions

If you're operating under a post-positivist approach, you'll want to advertise your study (maybe make a nice flyer), gather the names of everyone who agrees, and randomly select those who will be your participants. This works particularly well for teachers who are departmentalized (teach the same subject or content to different sections or classes, often found in upper elementary, middle, and high schools).

Take Amanda, for example. If she was going to use this approach to recruitment, the flyer in Figure 9.1 would serve to advertise her study. She would then randomly select the number

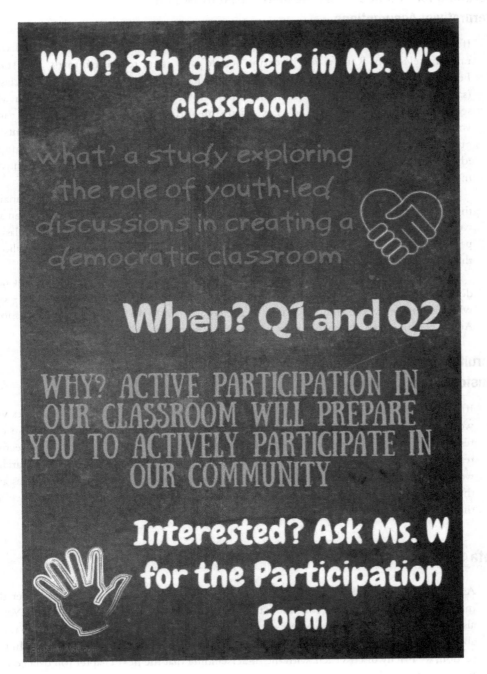

FIGURE 9.1 Amanda's Flyer

of youth to participate in her study. She would (ideally) select the same number of youth from each of her classes so that she spreads her participant pool across her classes. That's not how Amanda did move into spaces of participation with her youth, but it is one way to do so.

Recruiting for Practice-Based Research That Draws on Interpretivist Assumptions

If you're operating under the interpretivist approach, you will not be concerned with random selection. Rather, you'll recruit people who stand to most inform your study. For example, if Amanda was most interested in a particular group of youth in her classes (say, youth who seemingly are hesitant to participate in class discussions or youth who seemingly *love* to participate in class discussions), then she would only recruit those youth for her study. She would also recruit only from those youth whose parents or guardians have given consent (if she is required to get parental consent). She might identify those youth and approach them individually, handing them the flyer and inviting them to participate.

Likewise, she might only have one class in which she wants to work on democratizing their discussions (maybe her sixth-period class is the one she wants to start with). Then she would only recruit from that class, again, passing out her flyer and inviting the entire class to participate. If all 25 youth agree, she might want to choose purposefully (e.g., those who fit the description of who can best help her answer her research question).

A third option might be to recruit across her classes and then purposefully (versus randomly) select youth from across her classes. She might choose one or two from each class—one who seemingly loves to and one who is seemingly hesitant to participate in class discussions. Across her six classes, she would have selected between six and 12 participants.

Recruiting for Practice-Based Research That Draws on Transformative Approaches

If you're operating under the transformative approach, neither of the previous examples will work. That's because this approach requires you to involve your participants (who are co-researchers with you) from the onset of the design of your study. From this perspective, research should convoke the radical imagination of the people with whom the researcher works, which provides an opportunity for people to use research to improve their lives and the lives of those around them. Amanda White's study is a nice example of how she invoked the participation of her youth in her practice-based study.

Data Sources

As you continue to design your practice-based research study, you'll want to consider the many sources of data that can contribute to finding an answer to your research question. You'll also want to think about how you are going to manage your data. Finally, you'll want to think about the many analytic tools and resources for supporting you in analyzing your data. In this section, we briefly discuss each, with the understanding that the next chapter (on data collection and analysis) is a complementary chapter to this one.

There are many sources of data that you can consider for your practice-based research. If you are working in the interpretivist or transformative approaches, you're required to triangulate your data. That is, you'll select multiple sources from which your data will come, making your study more credible. If you are working in the post-positivist approach, you can select more than one data source for your study; just be sure you can analyze it in ways that map onto the standards of your approach.

Observations

Observations can be valuable sources of information for researchers. Observations in classrooms can be quite challenging because of the social nature of classrooms. As a teacher in the classroom in which your research is being conducted, you are an active observer—a researcher observing and recording all that is happening while you are participating in the study, making for a busy time for you! There are two ways to think about capturing observational data: with a research instrument or with you as a human instrument.

The first, using a research instrument, is probably the least challenging as most instruments appear in the form of a checklist or a counting (of sorts). Take, for example, a research instrument we designed, the TEX-IN3 (Hoffman, Sailors, Duffy, & Beretvas, 2004). The instrument contains three components: text inventory, in-use inventory, and text interviews. The text inventory included 17 different text types, with supporting rubrics that rate text quality. The second part, the observational in-use inventory, documents how children, youth, and their teachers are using the various forms of texts found inside their classrooms. The inventory includes three types of observations: the use of text in a particular subject area, the use of text among all students in the class, and the use of text by three specific students in the class. The data are compiled across the observations and are used to calculate a Quality Time Engaged (QTE) score, weighting text engagement with text quality. The text interviews were designed to capture and record the understanding, interpretations, values, and beliefs about the texts in the classroom. Observers rated the response of the students using a scale ranging from one (low understanding) to five (high understanding) and rated the teachers using a similar scale; additionally, teachers were asked to rank the various text types in their classrooms on a scale from one (most valuable) to 17 (least valuable).

While we used the instrument to demonstrate the importance of the text environment (from a social practice perspective) to growth in comprehension achievement, this particular instrument may not be one that works for your study, especially if comprehension instruction and your text environment are not the foci of your practice-based research study. Ours is not the only observational instrument available for research, obviously. There are many others that focus on literacy practices in classrooms. The nice thing about using a published instrument is that they have been validated. That is, they have been shown to measure what they say they are measuring and their scores are reliable. If you are interested in using an existing instrument for your research, you'll want to be sure it's reliable and valid (we cover these terms in the next chapter). You'll also want to be sure the instrument supports you in answering your research question.

The second way to approach observational data is by collecting data, taking a field notes approach. This positions you as a human instrument. The notes that you take will be highly focused, documenting data that support you in answering your research question. Obviously, the data collection will be done during the time that your focus practice is taking place.

Through field notes, we can document what is taking place, who is participating (and who is not), how children and youth are interacting with each other, what tools are being used and how, how bodies move through space and time with each other and the tools inside those spaces, and who is using those spaces and how, to name a few.

In the case of Amanda, she focused her observational field notes during literature circles, documenting the triads of youth as they were engaged with each other. She noted who was in each triad (youth had freedom to move between triads as they saw fit), what the nature of their conversation was, who was talking (and who wasn't), and what the text was that centered the conversation. She also supplemented her field notes with audio recordings of the conversations.

These audio recordings became data that supplemented her field notes. At the end of each day, she listened to the conversations of each focus triad (triads where members of her research team were found), noting who was taking the lead in the conversations and how each person was "taking up" the points in the discussion, how the youth transitioned between each other, and the role of the text in those "uptakes."

Other teachers make observations and jot notes throughout the day in a journal. At the end of the day, they "write around" those notes, drawing from both memory of the day and their responses to their observations. Teachers who engage in this type of journal note-taking find it a helpful way to keep up with their responsibilities of data collection while teaching and find that writing in their journal at the end of the day gives them insight they might not have while they are teaching.

Interviews

Like observations, interviews are another source of rich data for practice-based research. And, like observations, there are various ways to think about engaging in interviews. One is through one-on-one, semi-structured interviews and the other is through focus groups (using semi-structured questions).

One-on-one, semi-structured interviews are just what they sound like. These are ways of engaging with your participants so you can understand the attitudes, opinions, and beliefs (among other things) of your participants. Interviews can last any amount of time, but you'll want to plan to give plenty of time for your participants to reply to your questions at length. The tricky part of doing one-on-one, semi-structured interviews is when to do them. You need a quiet location (especially if you are going to audio record the interviews) and a (at least semi-) private space. Sometimes teachers invite their participants to have lunch with them and conduct the interview there. Other times, teachers interview their participants during downtime in classrooms.

Focus Groups

Focus groups are very similar to interviews (in their need for a quiet location and in that they are guided by questions that get at understandings of participants' beliefs, attitudes, and opinions). However, they are unique. Focus groups provide participants opportunities to talk about what's important to them and to build upon the responses of others in the focus group as this structure capitalizes on communication between participants. Rather than asking individual people to respond to a question, people are encouraged to talk to each other, exchanging stories and commenting on each other's perspectives and experiences. This allows for participants to explore and pursue their own priorities within a given topic.

Focus groups are generally between five and seven people. If you have more participants in your study than this, you might want to create several focus groups and meet with them separately. Or, you might want to sample from the larger group of participants and hold a single focus group, meeting with them over time, across your study. Your sampling could be homogeneous (e.g., people with shared experiences, such as youth from your second-period class only), or you might want to sample from across your participants (e.g., using random or volunteer sampling from across your classes).

Audio/Video Recording and Transcribing

One thing to consider as you are engaging in data collection is whether or not (and to what degree) you use audio or video recording to capture data. People often use these forms of data to complement their observations and interviews or focus groups so that they have a set of data that is more detailed than the notes they take during their field notes and interviews or focus groups. The upside of this is that the recordings are a form of reality that notes cannot possibly capture. The downside is that transcribing the data is extremely time-consuming.

That said, we have seen teachers use both audio or video recordings and transcriptions effectively as part of their practice-based research. For example, Ellen Webber video recorded her children during her read alouds so that she could later watch the transition from hand-raising to talking more realistically in her classroom. She did not need to transcribe her videos; rather, the videos served as a source of data that she could not capture while she was teaching. In her "marking" of her data (coding; see the next chapter), she noted the point at which children reverted to raising their hands and made note of what she said and how she invited her class into the read aloud, then started using that data to reframe her invitations into the read alouds.

Artifacts

Your classroom is chock-full of data sources waiting for you to identify them as such (e.g., work samples, journal entries, products created by your participants). In the research, those data sources are called *artifacts*. Artifacts are things that people, communities, and societies make for their own use. They are material evidence of actions and activities in classrooms, especially. Often, observational data involves the documentation of the creation of artifacts. Through analyzing an artifact, we can gain insight into the person who made it; how it was used; who used it; and the beliefs, understandings, and values people hold about it. Artifacts can stand as data sources in their own right and can serve as conversation starters for interviews.

Measures

Similar to the sheer number of artifacts found in classrooms today, so there are many measures that are generated on a regular basis. These measures are both formal and informal, formative and summative (e.g., reading and writing benchmarks, running records, end-of-unit assessments). These measures can be used for a design that documents growth over time or impact as a result of a shift in instruction. This would be a pre-/post-design, of sorts. We would encourage you to consider using existing measures where you can, but you might also want to create your own measure. If you do, you'll need to consider the validity and reliability of the instrument; we discuss each of these factors in the next chapter.

Similarly, there are other measures available that you will want to seek out, depending on the topic you are exploring in your practice-based research study. For example, if your project is focused on increasing the reading motivation of your youth, you might want to consider the Motivation to Read Profile—Revised (Malloy, Marinak, Gambrell, & Mazzoni, 2013) and the Me and My Reading Profile (Marinak, Malloy, Gambrell, & Mazzoni, 2015). The first measures motivation to read fictional text and the second, informational text; both have been validated and are reliable (Parsons et al., 2018).

Likewise, you might want to administer a survey to your class. For example, Amanda R. was curious as to how her youth were using the term *leadership*. She was concerned that her definition of the word was not necessarily aligned with theirs. So, she designed a survey and asked her students to complete it. The survey you design can be open-ended (as was Amanda's) or it can be based on a Likert scale, where one means one end of a spectrum and four means another. We recommend you have even-numbered scales for your

Pause and Reflect

- What data work best for your study? Observational data? Interview data? Artifacts? Measures?

- What challenges do you foresee with the various data sources? How can you overcome these challenges?

- Will you audio or video record as another source of data? If so, how will you use the data to support and complement other sources of data?

youth to choose from, as with odd-numbered scales people gravitate to the middle (e.g., on a scale of one to five, people will often choose a three).

Researcher Reflexivity

While not required in the post-positivist approach to research (seemingly because that type of research is neutral), interpretivist and transformative approaches require that researchers acknowledge their positionality going into and during the study. Positioning theory would suggest that we (as members of families, communities, and societies) take up particular positions (e.g., I'm a researcher. I'm a teacher. I'm a mother. I'm a sister.) and those positions allow us to see the world from the perspective of that position. Moreover, people in our communities assign positions to us that we may or may not wish to carry. Positions are different from roles: Roles are static and positions are more fluid. In fact, in our opening chapter, we asked you to take up the position of researcher and have positioned you as such throughout the chapters in this book. Our positions unfold through the various narratives and storylines that are both told by us (about ourselves) and told about us (by others).

To that end, the way we position ourselves and the way others position us (especially in the presence of our participants) have the potential to influence not only what data we collect, but how they are collected and how they are analyzed. It is important in the interpretivist and transformative approaches that we acknowledge our positionality through what is called researcher reflexivity. Throughout the decisions you make as you design your study as well as during the study itself, you must continuously explore your own assumptions and how those assumptions shape what you do. Centrally important in reflexivity is how our assumptions shape how we see and think about our data. It is through our open reflexivity (i.e., writing about it) that others can see how our situational understandings bear on the analysis of our data.

Ethics and Approvals for Your Research

Now that you have decided upon the approach you'll take to your research, the next thing to think about is what kind of access you have to the kind of people who will participate in your study (or co-research with you). *Access* is defined as "the appropriate ethical and academic practices used to gain entry to a given community for the purposes of conducting formal research" (Jensen, 2008, p. 2). We would add to Jensen's definition the appropriate moral obligations that we (as researchers) have to the people with whom we interact during our research, regardless of the research approach that situates our work.

Approval From an IRB

To that end, one of the first points to consider is gaining approval to conduct your research by the appropriate ethics committee(s). In higher education, ethics committees are called institutional review boards, or IRBs, and they are governed by federal laws that protect human research participants (as there are boards that govern the ethical treatment of animals, too). IRBs are authorized by the federal government to evaluate research proposals to ensure ethical research practices. IRBs were formed for the protection of humans—especially those who are vulnerable—after a series of egregious experiments done to Black men in Tuskegee, Alabama. If you are not familiar with this study, we highly recommend you familiarize yourself with it. As a result of this tragic treatment of people by the medical profession, the U.S. Department of Health and Human Services issued policies that IRBs must follow to maintain their approval status.

You will want to follow the procedures and protocols established by your local IRB. In many cases, the first step in seeking approval by your IRB is a training component. Those procedures usually culminate in the submission of a research proposal, copies of any research protocols that are to be used, copies of recruitment flyers or announcements, and so on. Our IRBs are very helpful and supportive of students who are submitting proposals for the first time. In subsequent sections, we outline the components typically found in an IRB submission packet.

As for ethics committees in PK–12 local education agencies, we have found (in our field-based research and working with graduate students conducting practice-based research as part of their coursework) that there are many variations. In some cases, school districts have boards (located within an office in central administration) that act in similar ways to those in higher education. In other cases, the superintendent must sign off and grant permission for research in the district. In still other cases, permission only must come from a school principal. If you are working in a school governed by a tribal council, they will also have policies and procedures that you will need to address in seeking their consent to conduct research in your classroom.

Regardless, it is up to you to know what is required in obtaining permission to conduct research in your classroom prior to beginning your research. Depending on your situation, you may need approval from your institute of higher education and then from your local school or school district. We seek approval from our respective IRBs when we teach courses where our students are engaged in practice-based research; our IRBs give us the stamp of "non-regulated" research and send us on our way. Our students then must visit with their principals to determine if their districts have an IRB committee (or another process for approving research) and follow the appropriate path for approval.

In the eResource (www.routledge.com/9780367177607), we outline those aspects that you will probably be asked to address in your IRB proposal. If your local school district has an IRB, much of this information will need to be addressed there, too. If your school district does not have an IRB, you may want to include as much of this as possible in the document you present your principal.

Values of Dignity and Respect

IRBs are guided by three assumptions, and their policies and practices follow. The first assumption is respect for human dignity. This is the notion that people should formally consent to participate in your research and they must be fully aware of the benefits and harm that are associated with it. The second assumption is that researchers should select a design that poses the least risk while maximizing benefits to participants. The third is the assumption of justice—that the risks and benefits of your research should not fall disproportionately on any one group (Haggerty, 2008).

While our IRBs cannot possibly evaluate us on whether or not we are treating people with respect, we (ultimately) know ourselves whether we are or are not. First and foremost, not only must we get consent from our IRB, local education agencies (including schools and districts), and tribal councils (where appropriate); we must also get consent from the parents and guardians of youth. In some cases, IRBs and local schools require signed consent forms. In other cases, IRBs and local schools only require that you notify parents or guardians that you are collecting data in your classroom. It's up to you to know what the requirements are and to follow them.

Once those consents are obtained or you notify, depending on your situation, we are of the firm opinion that children and youth must also give their consent to participate in research as we believe them to be sentient beings who should be making such decisions about their lives. Even in cases where our IRBs only

Pause and Reflect

- What are the ethical conditions under which you are working? Where are the ethics committees that you need to interact with?

- What local procedures and protocols must you follow to conduct research in your classroom?

- How do you view informed consent with the children and youth in your classroom?

require notification of youth that we are collecting data for a research study, we still believe that there should be an option for children and youth to verbally agree to be in our studies. And, yes, we're talking even about the youngest of children.

Creating conditions where people can interact with us in confidential and private ways is important. Similarly, we presume that our research with people (rather than on people) provides them with means to improve their lives and the lives of the children and youth with whom they work. We also believe that people with whom we do research should participate with us in the design of a study as we are committed to creating spaces where indigenous knowledge can lead our research. We believe our findings should not only be rigorous but should be presented in ways that fully reflect the lived realities of the people with whom we work in our research.

Limitations

All research studies struggle with limitations. There are no perfectly designed studies. *Limitations* refer to the features of the context that may influence the results that you don't have control over. What is important in designing your study is to recognize and be explicit about how the limitations must be interpreted in considering the findings. Let's say that you are engaged in a study in your classroom where you are encouraging translanguaging between Spanish and English as a language resource for your bilingual students in their talk and writing. You are fluent in the target language but are not a native speaker, nor do you identify as Latinx. You may believe that this could be a factor influencing your findings. Since you have no way to adjust this factor, all you can do is mention that this may be a factor that you could not explore in your study but is certainly deserving of further inquiry. The real error would be not being explicit about this kind of limitation in reporting your study.

Comments, Suggestions, Things to Consider

In this last section, we offer some lingering thoughts as you design your study and (possibly) prepare your proposal. Much of the writing you do for your proposal will become part of your final research report. Some of the writing will be refined as you consider the potential audiences for your work.

- Use the first person where you can. There is a tradition in the sciences to write in the third person as this is perceived as distant and more objective about your topic, thus presenting the author as an "expert." The field of education has moved away from this. We encourage you to find your voice and write to your audience. Your voice will shine through and identify you as an expert in your study.

- Write with passion about your intents and contexts. You are deeply invested in your work. But, be careful about your passion overcoming your science. Statements you make must be grounded in evidence. If you allow your voice to come through to your reader, your passion will, too.

- Clear writing matters. The more you work to make your writing clear, the clearer your writing and message will become to your reader. There is a tradition in research to use the biggest words possible. That is not necessary. Avoid jargon and try not to use colloquial language (other than when you might be quoting your participants, but that will come later in your findings). But, don't think you have to use as many multisyllabic words as possible to appear smart. If your writing is clear, your reader will thank you. Length and complexity are not the goal. Clarity is.

- Follow a format where you can. There are standards and expectations for information contained in study designs and proposals. And, while you can deviate from these, you want to stay as close to those standards as possible, at least in your initial writing. If it is helpful, find a mentor text that you can model for your design or study proposal.

- Think about design as building an argument. Is the design of your study compelling to you? Will it be compelling to an external audience?

Summary

We hope we have left you more excited about what you are doing than anything else. Designing a study is an important part of doing research. Not thinking through a study before you start it can have serious ramifications on the other side. What if once you've completed collecting your data, you realize you didn't collect the kind of data you need to answer your research question? One of the beautiful things about practice-based research is its recursive nature. Don't feel like you have to (with all absolutes) be locked into what you propose to do. Although you don't want to get halfway through your study and shift your topic, it would be quite normal to see a new data source that would contribute to your study. Or, you could come to a new understanding through one of the iterations that might shift the conversation of your next interview or focus group. The only thing you might need to do if you do make changes to your design is notify your IRB or school adminis-

Points to (Re)Consider

Return to the opening questions. With which approach do you most align yourself? How does that decision influence the design of your study?

trators. This is something you'll want to talk with them about as you submit your proposal—to what degree you can make changes while in the midst of your study, and when (and if) you need to notify them of the changes.

We hope this chapter moves you forward in your practice-based research. We hope you use it to invite others into this space with you, through dialogues, online communities, and talking with other teachers around you about your work.

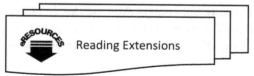

Reading Extensions

References

Bair, C. R. (1999). "Meta-synthesis." Paper presented at the 24th annual meeting of the Association for the Study of Higher Education, San Antonio, TX.

Bair, C. R., & Haworth, J. G. (2005). Doctoral student attrition and persistence: A meta-synthesis of research. In J. C. Smart (Ed.), *Higher education: Handbook of theory and research* (Vol. 19, pp. 481–534). Dordrecht, the Netherlands: Springer.

Haggerty, K. (2008). Institutional review board. In L. M. Givens (Ed.), *The Sage encyclopedia of qualitative research methods* (pp. 439–440). Los Angeles, CA: Sage.

Helin, J. (2013). Dialogic listening: Toward an embodied understanding of how to "go on" during fieldwork. *Qualitative Research in Organizations and Management, 8*(3), 224–241.

Hoffman, J. V., Sailors, M., Duffy, G. G., & Beretvas, N. (2004). The effective elementary classroom literacy environment: Examining the validity of the TEX-IN3 observation system. *Journal of Literacy Research, 36,* 303–334.

Jensen, D. (2008). Access. In L. M. Givens (Ed.), *The Sage encyclopedia of qualitative research methods* (pp. 2–3). Los Angeles, CA: Sage.

Ladson-Billings, G. (1995). But that's just good teaching! The case for culturally relevant pedagogy. *Theory Into Practice, 34,* 159–165.

Malloy, J. A., Marinak, B. A., Gambrell, L. B., & Mazzoni, S. A. (2013). Assessing motivation to read: The motivation to read profile-Revised. *Reading Teacher, 67,* 273–282. doi:10.1002/TRTR.1215

Marinak, B. A., Malloy, J. A., Gambrell, L. B., & Mazzoni, S. A. (2015). Me and my reading profile: A tool for assessing early reading motivation. *Reading Teacher, 69,* 51–62.

Parsons, A., Parsons, S., Malloy, J., Gambrell, L., Marinak, B., Reutzel, D., . . . Fawson, P. (2018). Upper elementary students' motivation to read fiction and nonfiction. *The Elementary School Journal, 118*(3), 505–523. https://doi.org/10.1086/696022

Sailors, M., Minton, S., & Villarreal, L. (2016). Literacy coaching and comprehension instruction. In S. Israel (Ed.), *Handbook of research on comprehension instruction* (pp. 601–625). New York, NY: Routledge.

10

Interacting With Your Data

Preview: This chapter extends and deepens the work you did in Chapter 9 with the design features of your study. This may be one of the more challenging chapters in this book. We will engage you in the work of practice-based researchers in gathering, analyzing, and interpreting data. We will take a fairly comprehensive perspective on data in research, and we will also encourage the researcher to be selective in the data collected for a study and methodical about how that data is analyzed. A little bit of good data, analyzed thoroughly, can go a long way toward a compelling argument in a well-designed study.

Consider the writing sample in Figure 10.1 that Hazel wrote to her father when she was five. Is this data? Could it be used as data? Under what conditions? For what purposes? What if it were part of a larger set of writing samples from Hazel over time, such as the ones presented in Figures 10.2, 10.3, and 10.4 (taken when she was two, six, and seven years old, respectively)? How does this make the data more interesting?

Points to Consider

What are you interested in studying? What are the concepts associated with what you are interested in studying?

What Is Data?

Most forms of scientific research are empirical in nature. *Empirical*, in a scientific research context, refers to things that can be observed or perceived and can be used as evidence in support of an argument. The observations we make, and our perceptions of the world around us, can be used to generate data. There is a general sense that data refers to numbers derived

FIGURE 10.1 Writing Sample—"Sorry for What I'm About to Do . . ."

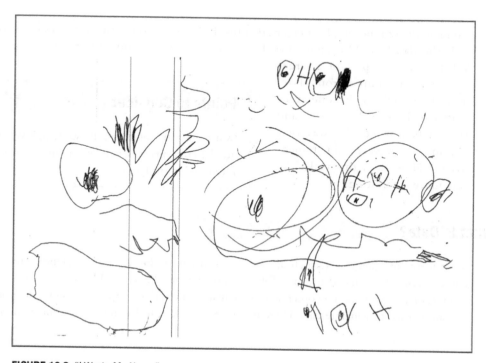

FIGURE 10.2 "I Wrote My Name"

FIGURE 10.3 "Do You Want to See My Dog?"

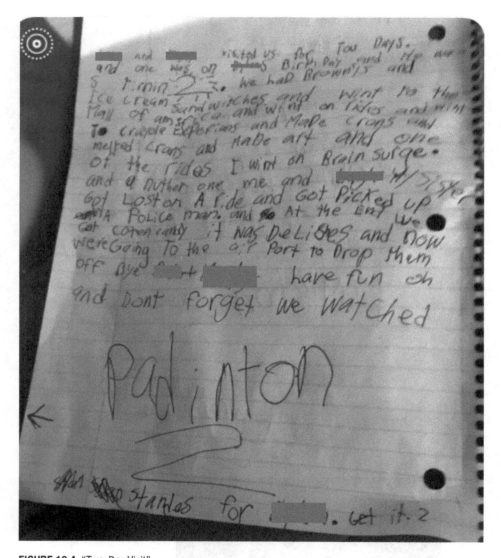

FIGURE 10.4 "Two-Day Visit"

from scores on some measures (e.g., tests). While this is one form that data can take, there are others, including answers to questions (e.g., in the form of interviews) and stories that people tell about themselves and others. Our focus in this book is on scientific research that draws on practice-based approaches.

Let's reconsider the data presented in Figure 10.1. It certainly meets the criterion of being observable, but is it being used as evidence in support of an argument? For a researcher investigating the forms, functions, and structures of emergent writing, this could become useful data in support of a position on development. The evidence in support of an argument would be strengthened with more examples over time, through conversations with the writer, and with direct observations of the writer while she (in this case) was writing.

Some researchers may choose to quantify this data in some way (e.g., counting the number of words, counting the number of words spelled conventionally, or applying a score for writing development based on a rubric for developmental forms of writing). The creation of numbers does not make the writing sample data. The original data is still the sample of writing. The numbers are extractions done for particular purposes (e.g., to aggregate performance across a large number of samples). With every transformation of data, there are risks of error and distortion (e.g., Is the rubric valid?) as well as of losing information (e.g., What is lost if we just give this writing sample a score of three?).

There is a misplaced belief that numbers, as data, are more objective, more trustworthy, and more important than other forms of data. This is false. And, none of the way the numbers are presented (really, even that which is measured), how they are presented, and how they are interpreted are objective at all. From a post-positivist perspective, the numbers generated around a student's performance on a standardized test are transformations from the marks the child made on a page in response to a particular probe (with the content and format predetermined). As a post-positivist researcher, one must go back to the original data and the conditions under which this data was gathered and transformed in order to make judgments about the quality of evidence that the data offers in support of an argument. Much of what we will consider in the next part of this chapter is focused on these considerations.

Studying Variables and Constructs

From a post-positivistic perspective, the answers to the questions in the "Points to Ponder" insert will generate a set of terms called *variables*. Figure 10.5 contains some research questions you might ask if you were interested in reading achievement from a post-positivist perspective.

- How can reading achievement be enhanced through concentrated work on vocabulary?
- What role can drama play in improving reading achievement?

FIGURE 10.5 Research Questions From a Post-positivist Perspective

Each of these questions can be answered with data that can be named and measured (e.g., reading achievement). These data are called *variables* because they can be measured, or assigned a value, and that value can vary. In research, variables can also be described in terms of the focus for a study. In post-positivist work, dependent, or outcome, variables are the focus (as in reading achievement). Independent (or predictor) variables are often the focus in a study in terms of how they influence (or can be manipulated to influence) a dependent or outcome variable.

From an interpretivist perspective, those same questions related to your research interest will also generate a set of terms. The answers to these questions will generate terms that are better described as *constructs* (e.g., identity, interests) than variables. Figure 10.6 contains some research questions you might ask if you were interested in reading achievement and were approaching your study from an interpretivist perspective.

- What role does a child's identity play in reading achievement?
- How do the interests of motivated readers compare to those of children who are seemingly unmotivated to read?

FIGURE 10.6 Research Questions From an Interpretivist Perspective

In a study that draws from the interpretivist paradigm, these types of constructs will probably not be quantified. Rather, they will be explored through talk, opinions, thoughts, beliefs, and stories that people tell. Similarly, there is less attention in interpretivist work to directionality (e.g., how vocabulary influences comprehension) and more attention to the immediate context and how different constructs interact with each other (e.g., motivation to read and its relationship to reader identity).

From a transformative perspective, the answers to these questions would not only look at constructs (such as identity) but also would include notions of power. Figure 10.7 contains some research questions you might ask if you were interested in reading achievement and were approaching your study from a transformative perspective.

- In socioeconomically diverse schools and/or districts, which children/youth carry the label "struggling reader"? Are there differences in the number of children/youth who carry that label across racial/ethnic groups?
- How do teachers in those schools position children/youth who are labeled as "struggling reader"? How do other children/youth position those who are labeled as "struggling reader"?
- How do children/youth who are labeled "struggling reader" position themselves as readers? As writers? As learners?

FIGURE 10.7 Research Questions From a Transformative Perspective

Practice-based research, because it is not methodologically bound to any one paradigm, can draw from data identified as variables and data identified as constructs. The most important thing to remember is that your data should be empirical, collected carefully and systematically, and analyzed thoroughly. We provide an explanation of each of these phases of working with data in the sections that follow. We've organized the sections around the various types of tools that are used in educational research because, no matter what paradigm you are operating under, tools are at the heart of data collection. While there has been a strong tradition in education to use the term *instrument* to describe what we use to collect data, we prefer the use of *tools* since it is more inclusive of all paradigms.

Gathering Data: Tools and Considerations in the Post-Positivist Paradigm

Regardless of the research perspective, you will rely on tools in your data collection. These tools are used to capture data for analysis. Stepping outside of education, think about a blood pressure monitor as a tool for assessing blood pressure. If you are an individual with high blood pressure, this tool is useful to you for data. If you are researcher looking at the relationship between changes in blood pressure and its relationship to heart attacks, this tool is useful to you. A test is a tool. An observation of a teacher is a tool. A rubric for scoring writing is a tool. The confidence you have in your findings and that your audience has for the evidence you gather in your research is dependent, in part, on the quality of the tool and your own skill in using that tool. In this section, we provide an overview of the various tools used to gather data from the varying research paradigms and those things that must be considered as you make choices about the tools you will use in your research.

In consideration of the quality of the tools used in studies, researchers commonly look at the reliability and validity of the instruments used in data collection. *Reliability* refers to consistency. A handheld stopwatch used for measuring a runner's speed in a 100-meter race is a tool. Five judges using stopwatches may actually come up with slightly different times for a runner. The differences may be related to the tool or to the skill of those using the stopwatches. You might increase reliability (reduce error) by deeper training of the judges or by insuring that all of the judges are using the same brand of stopwatch. You might eliminate the stopwatches and judges altogether and shift to an electronic measurement system. All of these are moves to increase reliability and therefore trust in the data that is generated by a tool. Achievement tests are tools. Do these tests yield consistent scores for the same person on the same construct? There are procedures for assessing the reliability of these tools that publishers gather as they develop these tests. There are some fairly easy steps to increasing the reliability of a test (e.g., generally increasing the number of items, using multiple tools to determine a score), but some of these come at a cost (e.g., more time required, expenses).

Validity addresses the question of how well a tool assesses what it claims to measure. A blood pressure monitor may be reliable in the score it generates, but that does not mean that it is valid for all purposes: Is blood pressure a valid measure of overall health? Or, along similar lines: Is a reading achievement test a valid measure of potential for success in college? You cannot prove a tool is valid. The best you can do is examine evidence and compose an argument for validity. In doing this work, researchers typically reference the types of validity found in Figure 10.8.

Content Validity	The content of a state assessment is mapped onto state curriculum standards.
Construct Validity	A tool to assess reading comprehension is designed around a theoretical model for reading.
Concurrent Validity	A tool is developed for measuring reading comprehension and it yields the same scores as a tool that is widely accepted and has been used in research before.
Predictive Validity	A tool is developed to predict reading success at the end of 3rd grade. Studies are done that demonstrate the relationship between the original test score and reading achievement at the end of third grade.
Consequential Validity	Valid for what? This is a cautionary path for tools that might be developed for one purpose and used from another. Is a 'valid' tool for accessing reading comprehension valid for use with English Language Learners? Is a valid tool for assessing high school graduation by meeting state standards also valid for college admission?

FIGURE 10.8 Types of Validity

Complications

A tool might have excellent support for reliability and validity, but there might be additional factors to consider. A rubric for the scoring of writing on a state test may have excellent qualities, but what if the individuals scoring samples using the rubric are not trained? A reliable tool with an unreliable scorer becomes unreliable and therefore invalid.

There are many situations in research where the researcher is actually the tool for data collection. A researcher observes in a classroom taking field notes. These field notes become data that is later analyzed. What evidence can be used to argue for the reliability and the validity of the field notes taken? Providing samples of field notes in a report is one option that allows the reader to examine the data being used for analysis.

Measurement

When numbers are assigned to data, the researcher must be considerate of the qualities of the data as they are used to represent those qualities. Numbers used to represent data tend to fall into certain scales. The scale for the data allows for certain kinds of analysis. The scales represented in Figure 10.9 are typically used in post-positivist research.

Nominal	Numbers assigned to data on this scale are mostly arbitrary and focus on identity. Party affiliation might be assigned as: 1 (democratic), 2 (republican), 3 (independent), 4 (other). These numbers can be used to divide of disaggregate data (e.g., Percent in favor of national health care by party affiliation). But the numbers cannot be averaged, for example, to represent anything.
	This is not to say that the creation of nominal scales is without problems. Why is gender represented so often as a binary? How do you represent ethnic or racial identity on a scale in school environments that are diverse? Where children come from multiracial families? Multilinguistic families?
Ordinal	Numbers assigned to data on this scale reflect both identity and magnitude. For example, in distinguishing the socio-economic status of parents a scale might be crated to divide low (1) from middle (2) from high (3) The assignment would be made based on consideration of factors such as education level and income level. In contrast to a number on a categorical scale, the value represents the amount of something moving from lower to higher. Often, as with categorical data, these divisions are used in the disaggregation of data (e.g., the percent distribution of party affiliation by SES status. The order of finish in a race is another example of the use of an ordinal scale. The numbers 1 (first), 2 (second), and 3 (third) tell us the order but nothing about the differences between the three.
Interval	Numbers assigned to data on this scale reflect identity, magnitude and equal intervals. Temperature in Fahrenheit can be considered as interval – where the 10 degree difference between 40 and 50 degrees is the same as the 10 degree difference between 60 and 80 degrees. Standardized scores on achievement tests are often regarded as on an interval scale.
Ratio	The numbers assigned to data on this scale reflect all the properties of the interval scale but have a meaningful value for zero. Weight is an example of a ratio scale. It is meaningful to describe something as having 0 weight. It is not meaningful to talk about a 0 as meaningful on a test score.

FIGURE 10.9 Measures

The consideration of scales is important in planning for any kind of statistical analyses with data. For example, it is reasonable to calculate averages for data on an interval scale or higher, but not on the lower scales. With numbers on an ordinal scale, it is more appropriate to display data as, for example, the number of first-place, second-place, or third-place finishes in footraces. You could average the running times in those races (e.g., average time on a 100-meter race). This is the difference in scales.

These scaling issues become important as you analyze and interpret numerical data. Consider an assessment tool that relies on a Likert scale for reading attitude. We can create a four-point scale (e.g., "'I enjoy reading outside of school.' Mark one of the following: (1) not at all, (2) a little, (3) quite a bit, (4) very much"). Is the data that comes from this measure on a nominal, ordinal, interval, or ratio scale? Most people would regard these kinds of data as ordinal. But there are occasions where researchers regard these data as interval and thus create average scores on reading interests.

Selecting Tools

The researcher faces the challenge in selecting tools that relate to the variables or constructs under scrutiny in a study. Practice-based researchers may draw on tools that reflect numerical transformations of data or other approaches. Very often, the questions posed by practice-based researchers require that we use combinations of these approaches.

Numerical data may be as simple as counting events (e.g., the number of times a child chooses to read during "free time" in the classroom; the number of times a child asks a question inside of a book club discussion; book check-out frequency, by genre, from the library). These can be powerful measures in relation to research questions that are looking toward the effects of some kind of intervention.

Numerical data may also be derived from such sources as surveys, questionnaires, or tests. You may have access to data that is already being collected (e.g., book circulation from the library, end-of-unit assessments provided by textbook publishers, school district or state assessments). These data can be very useful as much of the work on reliability and validity for these instruments has already be done. Numerical data may also be derived from observation instruments that have a predetermined structure (e.g., types of questions asked by a teacher, amount of time devoted to the various components of a mini-lesson).

You may locate instruments in the research literature that have been used in previous studies. Some of these might be commercially produced; others may have been developed locally. You might take an instrument and modify it for your own purposes. A simple example of this is the Garfield assessment of reading attitudes. This tool has been used widely in research exploring reading. Here again, much of the work on reliability and validity for this instrument has already been done. Using existing instruments will also a provide another path back into the existing literature. For example, searching on

Pause and Reflect

If your practice-based research project draws from traditions of post-positivism, what tools might you use for data collection that will support you in answering your research questions? What considerations must you make in selecting those tools? Will they be published tools or ones you create as part of your research?

Google Scholar for "Garfield assessment of reading attitudes" will take you to the source article (McKenna & Kear, 1990), the 822 other publications that have cited this work, and a whole set of other publications related to this topic.

Numerical data may be derived from analytical tools used in research. For example, there are numerous scales for evaluating writing samples. These can range from holistic scales to analytic scales. The scoring of writing samples using scales that assign a numerical score to a writing sample can be problematic. Careful attention must be given to the training of how to score those writing samples. The good news is that with this kind of scoring, you can have multiple people scoring independently; looking across these scores for consistency can then provide some confidence in the data as reliable.

In the end, your focus may be so specific that you need to develop your own instruments to reflect your purposes and your context. In the previous chapter, we described our research into drama pedagogies and comprehension. We developed all of the instruments for this study on our own. This can be a challenging path as the burden is on the researcher to demonstrate the reliability and validity characteristics of these tools.

Gathering Data: Tools in the Interpretivist and Transformative Paradigms

To reiterate, non-numerical data is still empirical and meets the criteria for scientific research. In drawing on this data, the researcher becomes a part of the tool set. It is important to represent yourself and the data collection procedures you use in your work as transparent and trustworthy. We offer some summaries of approaches that have been used widely in research. Consider this as a starting place and not a full list of the tools that can be used.

Research Tools

Both preestablished (and published) instruments and open-ended field notes are important sources of data for practice-based research. While we provided an overview of each in Chapter 9, here we provide a more nuanced look. There are as many research instruments available for use as there are topics being explored in educational research. These research instruments began finding their way into research on teaching in the 1960s. One of the earliest of those studies (Flanders, 1970) was interested in how "talk" in classrooms reflected "democratic" or "authoritative" structures. With his work, Flanders developed an observation system called the Flanders' Interaction Analysis Categories (FIAC), commonly known as "the Flanders system." The FIAC was designed to capture verbal "behaviors" and to be inclusive of all possible communication interactions in classrooms. During the next several decades, many observation systems were developed that focused on documenting teacher "behaviors" and then correlating them with student outcome measures. Although many of these, and of those developed since then, yield rich insight into classroom teaching and learning, they can be cumbersome for teachers to use in their classrooms.

There are several observation tools available to you, depending on the nature of your practice-based research project. One such tool that works well for classroom teachers (who are interested in documenting the nature of the interactions in their classrooms, for example) is the Dialogic Inquiry Tool (DIT; Reznitskaya, 2012). In her work, Reznitskaya designed the DIT to describe and analyze teacher–student interactions as a way of supporting teachers as they rethink the quality of talk during literature discussions. Teachers can either videotape or observe in real time segments of classroom interactions (e.g., 20 minutes each) and systematically study the discourse patterns between the teacher/youth and youth/youth. Evangelina Muniz used this instrument in her practice-based research study; it supported her in thinking about how she and the young people in her classroom interacted with each other.

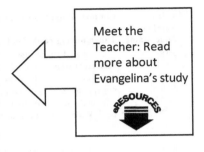

Meet the Teacher: Read more about Evangelina's study

Field Notes

Taking field notes, drawing on traditions from anthropology (e.g., ethnography), is common in practice-based research. This is not the same as observing using a fixed structure (e.g., as in an evaluative observation from an administrator following a format). The structure for field notes can vary, but generally the observer writes in narrative form, recording as much as possible regarding the actions and words observed. These notes can be enhanced if the observation has supporting audio or video recordings. Typically, field notes are reviewed as soon as possible, with the researcher adding notes on patterns observed in a side-column format. These researcher notes are the first step in moving toward analysis.

Some would say that observation notes are biased toward those things the researcher is focused on as well as implicit beliefs and values. We agree and believe that the researcher reflexivity statement (see Chapter 9) allows for the transparency required in addressing those biases and beliefs. The researcher needs to be transparent about these influences in sharing data from observations. Two people observing the same set of events may have similar field notes, but there will still be differences. This is in part due to the differences in the perspectives that researchers bring to field-based data. If you are attempting to establish consensus related to your observations (akin to reliability in post-positivist research), you can do so by engaging in observations with your research team members (or other teachers at your school who are also doing practice-based research) and debriefing afterward concerning the things that were the focus of the observation, and how those things were represented in the field notes. We offer a sample of a set of field notes from Sue Anne Umpierre's practice-based research study in Figure 10.10.

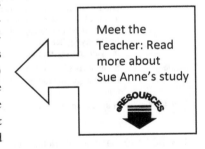

Meet the Teacher: Read more about Sue Anne's study

Notice these observational notes were taken from video logs Sue Anne took as she was studying the ways in which she could make her classroom more dialogic. She originally tried to observe "on the spot" but found that she had to make choices between teaching and writing, and teaching won. As a result, she video recorded her teaching and, at the end of the day, went back and watched the video, stopping to note in her observation log those places in the video that were most relevant to her study. For example, you'll see in the figure that she noted data points at time stamps 0:18, 0:52, 1:11, 1:32, 1:57, 2:46, and so on. It's not that the other things that happened in between those stamps are not important; it's just that they were not relevant to her research question.

Video Number / Time Stamp	Context: What I Observe	Code for Observation	My Interpretations/Impressions
	Taken during read aloud (video)		
0:18	"I asked students to share with each other what they think or predict the story to be about	Encouraging open discussion	
0:52	"I am going to take you back to your dialogic classroom norms so..." We read them together.	Traditional approach	The use of I is authoritative. When I said that I am going to take you back to "your" norms, I took myself out of the process. A dialogic stance includes the teacher as part of the dialogue.
1:11	"We all agreed on these norms when we made them right?"	Traditional approach	Ended with an Authoritative stance, with the use of "right?" I put myself back into the process as I referred to the norms as ours, but ruined it with, "right?"
	"So, when I ask a question, it doesn't mean you have to answer it to me. When we have our discussions and I say share your thoughts, instead of looking at me, look to each other"	Encouraging open discussion but still traditional approach	Authoritative stance due to "I say"
1:32	"If Jason is talking, we are all going to look at Jason. And whatever Jason says, you can go on what he says, so if he sparks something in your imagination you can comment on him"	Encouraging open discussion but still traditional approach	Authoritative stance due to "We are all going to..."
1:57	"I took away the teacher authority chair, instead of being that teacher where you have to answer to me, we are trying to have that dialogue where we are talking to each other."	Encouraging open discussion but still traditional approach	Authoritative stance due to "I took away.."
2:46	I ask a question. Students start to answer to me. I direct students to "not look at me, but to look at each other"	Encouraging open discussion	
2:54	A student (Matthew) is leaning onto the table. He is blocking another student from seeing me and another student. I ask him to check his body language. I ask if he is leaving her out. I answer yes for you and say that I do it, too.	Encouraging open discussion but still traditional approach	Authoritative stance due to asking him to check his body language and "I answer for him".
3:06	Students begin to talk towards me, I encourage them to talk to each other	Encouraging open discussion	
4:04	"I am going to ask you to read"	Traditional approach	I was taking traditional approach. Not convoking imaginations

FIGURE 10.10 Sample Field Notes From Sue Anne's Classroom

Sue Anne organized her observation notes in four columns: (a) video number and time stamp, (b) context: what she observed, (c) code for observation, and (d) her interpretation. The first is self-explanatory. The second was her direct transcription of the video she used to capture her observation. The third was the code she used to identify those places where she was using either traditional or more encouraging approaches to dialogue. The fourth column was her interpretation of her observations based on her goals for her study.

Sue Anne's data collection method is but one way to go about documenting her practice. Her design to gather one set of data in the way she did was chosen because she was particularly interested in her role as the teacher in setting the learning environment and either making her classroom more dialogic or closing down opportunities to dialogue. By videotaping her interactions with her youth and watching and coding those videotaped interactions, Sue Anne was able to revisit her teaching and think through the interactions. This was one of her earliest entries into data collection and one of several data sources for her practice-based research study.

Gathering People's Stories and Insights

While observations and artifacts can give you access to data that will support you in answering your research question, this data can only inform what you see, not what people with whom you work are feeling. You can gather the insight of people with whom you work through talking with and listening to them. This is typically done through interviews or focus groups.

Engaging in Research with Children and Youth

In addition to the commonplace survey data that children and youth gather during school-based research projects, it is important that we offer opportunities for children and youth to engage in data collection that is oriented toward interpretivist and transformative paradigms. In order to do so, we might

- Provide opportunities for (and encourage) young people to ask research questions that beg for data to be collected via interpretivist and transformative methods;

- Provide them with the tools to collect this type of data (e.g., audio recorders, transcribing software); and

- Teach them the ethics of collecting this type of data.

Interviews

Researchers may interview individual youth with structured or semi-structured formats. Structured questions are those that are both predetermined and asked of all participants. There is little flexibility in the way a researcher presents a question. Semi-structured questions are a combination of predetermined questions plus follow-up probes that allow you to ask participants to clarify ("Might you clarify what you meant when you said . . .?") and extend ("Might you say some more about . . .?") their responses.

The questions that you ask in your interviews should be open-ended rather than *yes/no* or leading (e.g., "You like our new approach, don't you?"). Some open-ended questions might start with stems such as, "Tell me how you're feeling about . . .", "Tell me what you think about . . .", "Talk with me about the changes we've made in our classroom . . .", or "What are you thinking we should do next?" You can feel free to ask follow-up questions that either clarify a response or extend a response. One thing we have found helpful in engaging our participants in interviews is to make eye contact, smile, and nod your head encouragingly. Sometimes people need affirmation in interviews; try not to evaluate their responses. Rather, nod your head encouragingly and use a placeholder such as, "Mm-hm." That's often enough to keep people talking.

Focus Groups

As we pointed out in Chapter 9, focus groups are another excellent way to collect data mainly because they create opportunities for people (your participants or co-researchers) to interact with each other. Focus groups are generally between five and seven people. If you have more participants in your study than this, you might want to create several focus groups and meet with them separately. Or, you might want to sample from the larger group of participants and hold a single focus group, meeting with them over time, across your study. Your sampling could be homogeneous (e.g., people with shared experiences, such as youth from your second-period class only), or you might want to sample from across your participants (e.g., using random or volunteer sampling from across your classes).

We typically ask for volunteers and we typically seat people in a circle when we use focus groups in our research. We explain the purpose of the focus group and encourage people to talk to each other rather than to us. We put forth general questions ("How are you feeling about . . .?" or "Let's talk about some of the experiences you've had thus far . . .") and take a backseat approach (watching, taking notes, etc.) so that the conversation can stem naturally within the group. Sometimes we find we have to step in and encourage the "quiet" people to contribute ("We'd love to hear what you're thinking . . .") or encourage debate and dialogue (to someone other than the speaker: "What do you think about what they said?"). When people agree or disagree, we use that as a point to ask people to expand on their thinking ("Might you say a little more about that for us?").

Amanda White used focus groups in her practice-based study. In fact, she and the youth in her classroom successfully used focus groups to support their efforts to democratize their eighth-grade classroom. If you're interested in using interviews or focus groups for your research, Figure 10.11 contains helpful tips for both.

- Ensure that the interview/focus group session is relaxed.

- The participant should be doing most of the talking. You are listening and taking notes.

- Ask clarification questions and/or questions that extend the responses of your participant(s).

- Try not to interrupt.

- Ask for concrete details and/or stories (where appropriate).

- Follow your hunches.

- Smile. Use laughter accordingly.

- Be okay with silence. Sometimes people need time to gather their thoughts before they respond.

FIGURE 10.11 Helpful Tips for Interviews and Focus Groups

Both focus groups and interviews can be transcribed; there are several ways to go about doing this. Some people like to transcribe only the parts of their data that are most salient to their research questions. This is similar to what Sue Anne did with her observational data (as described in Figure 10.10). Other people transcribe all of their interview and focus group data.

Regardless, researchers approach their data using what is known as "naturalized" or "denaturalized" transcription processes (see the work of Bucholtz, 2000). Naturalized transcription occurs when written language features (commas, periods, paragraphing, etc.) are inserted into spoken language as part of the transcription process. In other words, the naturalized transcriptions are "literacized." Denaturalized transcription maintains the features of oral language, such as "ums" and "ers." Denaturalized transcriptions can be difficult to read but may yield data that naturalized transcriptions do not. It is important to know what analytic approaches you will use with your data before you begin the transcription process as you will want to prepare your data (via transcription) for that process.

Teacher Reflection/Reflexivity Journals

Another systematic way to capture data for your practice-based research study is through regular entries in a journal. Journals are used quite frequently in educational research as they provide firsthand evidence of an event. Journal entries can be framed as a retelling of events or topics or as memoir-like. Not only do journals document events and activities (usually through observations); they often reflect the emotions (feelings and reactions) involved in the activities and events. Some people believe journals to be "too subjective," but reflective writing can facilitate reflective processes, and thus, they become not only a source of data but a space in which you can make sense of your data.

Sue Anne supplemented her observational field logs with journal entries. Figure 10.12 is a sample from one of her observational field logs. You might notice that the journal was accompanied by another source of data, an image of a physical artifact from her classroom; see the next section.

Artifacts of Teaching and Learning

It is quite common in educational research (especially practice-based research) to use the products or artifacts associated with teaching as data. We have already described the application of rubrics for scoring writing as an example of this kind of work in generating numerical data. But rubric-generated data is not the only artifactual data you might use as a data source. There are many more! Artifacts can be inclusive of the policies that guide the work you're asked to do in your classroom, the curriculum (and sometimes teacher guides) that you are given, and the historical documents that represent the school/system in which you participate.

In fact, if you look around your room at the sheer number of texts generated by you and your youth, you will get a good sense of the hundreds of artifacts to which you have access. In addition, documents you have created are also artifacts, including your lesson plans, anchor charts, writing samples that you share with your youth, and more. While it is not an exhaustive list, the 17 different text types that we identified in our earlier work (Sailors & Hoffman, 2014) might be used to get you started as you think about the various

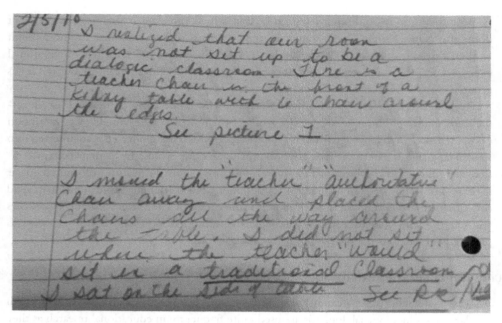

FIGURE 10.12 Observational Field Log From Sue Anne's Classroom

types of artifacts produced in your classroom. Figure 10.13 lists those text types and gives a brief description of each.

Digital images of your artifacts can help you record those artifacts. And, artifacts can be used to supplement other data sources. Figure 10.14 contains an image that accompanied Sue Anne's journal; she referred to this image in her journal entry in Figure 10.12.

Pause and Reflect

If your practice-based research project draws from traditions of the interpretivist perspective, what tools might you use for data collection that will support you in answering your research questions? If your practice-based research project draws from traditions of the transformative perspective, what role do your youth play in data collection?

Data Organization: Storing and Managing Data

Just as you organize the tools you use in your classroom for your daily practice, you'll want to have a plan for organizing the data you collect for your study. Organizing your data is important because you want to keep your data safe and maintain the ethical considerations of handling data (see Chapter 9). Some questions to ask yourself as you prepare for and engage in data collection include the following:

- What data will you have? You may end up with responses to surveys that you've administered that are stacked somewhere on your desk, scores on measures of assessments

Text types and examples	Explanation
Assessments: End-of-book tests, spelling and grammar tests, portfolios, etc.	Includes tests or testing materials used by the children in the classroom. These may appear as testing protocols from formal or informal assessments. Assessments are used for a variety of instructional purposes and goals.
Digital: Email, browser-based texts, reading and authoring applications, tests or test preparation, recorded books, news, text messaging systems, etc.	Includes any texts that are accessed and used through a digital medium.
Extended Text Process Charts: Inquiry charts, language charts, math or reading strategies, rubrics, writing process charts, etc.	Appear as connected texts (multi-sentence) that are usually procedural and guide readers and writers toward the use of a particular process or strategy.
Games/ Puzzles/ Manipulatives: Board games (Bingo, Clue), word sorts, magnetic poetry, etc.	Includes games designed for student use (often as independent or small group work) and feature text prominently.
Instructional Aids: Morning messages, labels, vocabulary lists, word banks, color charts, science/ math posters, etc.	Often public and often appear as a poster. They are always used to support instruction or represent past instruction. Often these instructional aid charts are used as a visual aid to support direct instruction or mini-lessons.
Journals: Reading response logs, personal and/or writing journals, content logs (inquiry in the subject areas), etc.	Often "local" texts created by the children based primarily on their work and writing. "Spiral folders" where children record their work in response to assignments may be considered in this category.
Leveled Books: Basal readers, "little books," guided reading books and decodable readers, etc.	Often found in "book format", but they differ from trade books because they are created explicitly for instruction and are leveled for difficulty and accessibility.
Limited Text Process charts: Alphabet charts, word walls, etc.	Include letter/word level texts that are procedural and guide the students in the use of a particular strategy or set of strategies. These are similar to the Extended Text Charts in purpose and design; however, they tend to focus at the letter or word level.
Organizational/Management Charts: Work boards, class rules, local or state curricular objectives, multiplication facts charts, student helper charts, etc.	Often used to manage or organize the social, academic, or curricular work within the classroom. They may be enlarged or small, local or public.
Reference materials: Thesaurus, globes, maps, atlases, dictionaries, encyclopedias, etc.	Used as resources for finding information (e.g., word spellings; locations; how to do something).

FIGURE 10.13 Text Types Typically Found in Classrooms

Serials: Scholastic newspapers, Ranger Rick, Highlights, classroom news reports, school newsletters, etc.	Often found moving in and out of a classroom on a regular basis.
Social/ personal/ inspirational displays: Child-of-the-week poster, "Readers, Read!", etc.	Used to motivate and inspire. They may come from a commercial source or they might be created locally.
Student/ Teacher published works: Student-authored books, reports from inquiry projects, text innovations, etc.	Usually locally authored books or publications that are on display and accessible for children to read.
Textbooks: Content area books (science, social studies, math, handwriting, etc.)	These literacy tools are texts that are typically identified with a subject/content area that are typically leveled by grade and the difficulty levels increase with each grade level.
Trade books: "Library books" (picture books, chapter books, poetry, etc.)	Typically found in "book format" and do not have any obvious instructional design features
Work Product Displays: Writing samples, tests, etc.	Displayed teacher or the work of children that is being "celebrated" and set forward for others to read and enjoy.
Writing on Paper: Story and sentence starters, reading/ math/ phonics/ spelling worksheets, etc.	Conceptualized on a continuum ranging from tightly constrained text response formats (e.g., check marks, fill in the blank, multiple choice) to entirely open-ended response/writing formats (e.g., blank paper, lined-paper).

FIGURE 10.13 (Continued)

FIGURE 10.14 Image of an Artifact From Sue Anne's Classroom

that are listed in your school's online grading system, and audio-recorded interviews with your participants. We recommend that you keep a master list of the data you have, when and where it was collected, where it is located, and any special notes you want to remember about it (e.g., the context under which it was generated and collected). You may find this master file helpful when you start to pull your data together for analysis.

- Will your data be physical or digital? While we collect both types of data (e.g., student work samples that are completed using physical materials), we tend to digitize all of our data so that it is all in one place. We recommend that you consider doing the same. Most smartphones today take very high-quality images; you can use your smartphone to digitize your data using the camera app or an app that converts physical data into a PDF or JPEG file.

- How will you keep that data safe and organized? The last thing you want is lost or damaged data. We recommend physical files be stored in a drawer or compartment dedicated only to the data you are using for your study. You might dedicate a digital file specifically for digital data you collect. We like to digitize all our data and store it together in a folder, with sub-folders for each type of data (or each participant, if that works better for you).

- Will you have backup copies of your data? We do because we have each suffered through the loss of data because we did not take proper precautions to have backup copies. As a result, we store copies of those digital files in several places, including on our laptops (which are encrypted so as to protect our data) and on cloud storage systems (Google Drive and our university clouds), in case something were to happen to our laptops (such as the time one of our laptops took a coffee bath). Your school district or employer might have specific guidelines for where you can store your data since some of it may be protected by the Family Educational Rights and Privacy Act (FERPA). This is a question you might want to ask as you are designing your study (see Chapter 9).

These questions are intended to help you think about how best to prepare your data so that you can move into data analysis easily and with no tears over lost or damaged data that might not be re-creatable.

Moving From Analysis to Interpretation

In this next section, we delve a bit deeper into the ways in which you might approach and analyze your data. As we did in earlier sections, we have organized this section by the various types of data you have collected. Typically, researchers talk about their analytic approach to their data. These approaches can be post-positivist in nature (i.e., you will use statistical analysis to analyze your data) or they can be more constructivist in nature (i.e., you will use constructivist methods to analyze your data). Many practice-based studies use both kinds of analysis in building an evidence-based argument.

There are a few important things to remember from this section. First, you'll want to be systematic with your data and to follow the norms associated with each of the approaches to data analysis. Each research paradigm (and the community that uses those paradigms) has certain expectations and norms that are expected to be followed. We present a few of those later. You may also want to keep your mentor texts close to you as you move forward in your analysis.

Similarly, the theory that you use to inform your study becomes very important in your analysis. You might think about a theory as a light that you shine on your data (Unrau, Alvermann, & Sailors, 2019) that will help you "see" it a bit more clearly. Or, you might think about theories as lenses through which we look as we describe the world. While it was not required in earlier paradigms of educational research to report your theory, the interpretivist and transformative theories do require that researchers report the theory that "drove" their study.

Numerical Data Analysis and Interpretation

Statistical analyses can be daunting. The major complications around statistical analyses, however, tend to involve large data sets and making inferences from a sample to a population. This kind of analysis is rare in practice-based research. In practice-based research, we are attempting to represent only the individuals or groups we are studying. Straightforward analyses involving frequencies, distribution patterns, and averages will often suffice.

Typically, the kinds of comparisons we make in practice-based research are across time periods. We look at baseline data as compared to end-of-study data. We might look at multiple data-collection points that correspond to iterations in particular interventions following a design-development perspective. For example, a teacher is working to strengthen the qualities of argument in students' writing. One way the teacher is collecting data is to construct a rubric for scoring writing that is sensitive to the elements of argumentative writing. The teacher works to insure the validity of the instrument and the reliability of scoring. The teacher assesses writing multiple times in the study corresponding to different modifications made (e.g., baseline, intervention one around feedback to students, intervention two focused on mentor texts, intervention three focused on peer feedback). The teacher may average scores within these periods for the class or may display individual scores of students in these periods.

Building an argument around these kinds of comparisons can be difficult. There are competing threats to explain the changes in performance that may not be related to the interventions. Are the students just growing normally over this time period of the study? Are the students becoming more sensitive to the measures you are using and learning to respond accordingly but not really becoming more powerful writers? Perhaps there were some other influences that were co-occurring with your planned interventions (e.g., the students were reading more informational text during this same time period)? Perhaps the score differences are just a matter of error of measurement? No study can anticipate all counter-interpretations, but the more the design of the study anticipates these counter-explanations, the more powerful an argument can be built. At a minimum, we suggest multiple measures that include both numerical and non-numerical data. There is always the option of using a comparison, or control, group: a group that is assessed but not exposed to the interventions you implemented. You should not let the absence of a comparison group, however, discourage you from doing practice-based research or thinking that without a control group you have no evidence in support of your claim. Replication of your research, by you or others, is just as powerful as, if not far more powerful than, comparison to a control group.

Interpretivist and Constructivist Analysis

Transcripts of interviews, field notes on observations, and documents written by students can be analyzed in a variety of ways. While there are software programs that can assist in this kind of analysis, we will focus on four basic strategies that are useful in moving from analysis to interpretation of data. There is the presumption in all of these strategies that different researchers applying the same strategies would come to similar interpretations.

Content Analysis

This analytic strategy is low-inference and works best when there is a specific focus. For example, you might be interested in the number of times that students ask a question in class discussion that is open-ended. In content analysis, you would search the data for instances of these kinds of questions. You might tally the number of different students and the patterns over time (possible increases). You might be interested in the use of multisyllabic words as an indicator of vocabulary growth. You might be interested in the use of metaphors in writing samples. Content analysis focuses on counting and distributions. For a more detailed description of the processes associated with content analysis, see Hoffman, Wilson, Martinez, and Sailors (2011).

Constant Comparative Analysis

This is an analytic strategy associated with grounded theory. It requires higher levels of inference than content analysis and presumes that the interpretations emerge through the data analysis and not from predetermined categories. In this analysis, the researcher makes multiple passes through the data looking for patterns that might be important and related to the research questions. In the initial set passes, the researcher uses what is referred to as *open coding*. Next, the researcher begins to "name" the patterns found in the open coding. These named coding categories lead to another round of coding using these categories (sometimes called axial codes). Here the researcher is looking for patterns in the data around these categories. The constant comparative analysis, in contrast to content analysis, is less focused on frequencies and distributions than it is on larger patterns and themes.

Discourse Analysis

This analytic strategy focuses on language in use. Discourse analysis may be used to examine a written text or a transcribed text from an oral interaction. Discourse analysis attends to the ways in which language governs how people interact with each other, as in the examination of turn-taking. Critical discourse analysis focuses on the ways in which the language choices and moves made reveal power relationships. If the researcher is interested in the participation of girls in book discussions, then a critical discourse analysis of a transcript might reveal the mechanisms that operate to exclude or marginalize the girls in the discussion. Who is talking the most? The least? What patterns of interaction between youth do you observe? How much "teacher talk" is there during interactions with youth? These are the types of questions you can answer using discourse analysis.

This is a short list of common types of analysis you can use if you are framing your study using an interpretive lens. There are others. Two excellent sources for analytic tools used in literacy research are *Literacy Research Methodologies* (Duke & Mallette, 2011) and *New Methods of Literacy Research* (Albers, Holbrook, & Flint, 2013).

Transformative Analysis

Analytic tools used in the spirit of transformative research can draw from both post-positivist (although this is less common) and interpretivist (more common) methods. However, one of the main differences in analysis from a transformative perspective is that the analysis relies heavily on particular theoretical frames to inform it. These might include queer theories, postcolonial theories, critical race theories, Marxism, DisCrit (critical disability studies), intersectionality, and Chicana feminism, to name a few. Several excellent resources for analytic tools used in transformative research can be found in *Understanding Critical Race Research Methods and Methodologies: Lessons From the Field* (DeCuir-Gunby, Chapman, & Schutz, 2018) and *Transformative Research and Evaluation* (Mertens, 2009).

To get you started, we've summarized a few methods used within this perspective. While there are many more, these are often used in action research, participatory research, youth participatory research, and practice-based research.

Narrative and Counternarrative Analyses

At its roots, narrative analysis stems from narrative inquiry, a way of thinking about people's experiences within a particular phenomenon, over time, and within larger social and institutional contexts. Narratives are the stories people tell about themselves, others, and the relationships in which they find themselves. From an analytic perspective, there are several different ways to analyze a narrative. Perhaps the most common is to use interviews and conversations (or interviews as conversations) as a starting point for data collection (Clandinin & Caine, 2008, p. 542). There are two basic ways of thinking about the analysis of a story. The first, thematic, interrogates what a story or group of stories is about. The second, structural, pays attention to how a story is composed and what its aims and goals are based on how it is told (Riessman, 2008, p. 539).

Framed from a critical perspective, counterstories (or counternarratives, as they are commonly called) are narratives that shatter the widely held beliefs and "truths" that are told about people, communities, and cultures. These stories "counter" the Grand Truths that the dominant culture holds about people who are marginalized.

Critical Discourse Analysis

This analytic strategy grew out of the spirit of discourse analysis, which centers on the qualitative analysis of spoken or written texts but differs in its examination of the often-subtle ways language reproduces and maintains unequal power relations. Interestingly, studies that use critical discourse analysis (CDA) as a method attempt to "capture the interconnections among discourse, power, and social organization" (Weninger, 2008, p. 145), making it an exceptional method for practice-based research that promotes double-loop reflection. If you are interested in examining the discourse patterns in your classroom with a particular focus on who gets to talk, when, and under what conditions (and your frame is from a feminist or critical race perspective), then CDA would work for you. In the spirit of transformative research, you would not just stop when you have the answers to these questions—you would do something to equalize the inequity you very likely will find. That's the *doing* part of practice-based research.

(Critical) Arts-Based Methods

Drawing from the field of arts-based inquiry, which centers affective and emotive responses to experiences, senses, and bodies (Finley, 2008, p. 143), critical arts-based (CAB) inquiry also borrows from various forms of art as part of the research process, including narrative writing, drama, poetry, videography, photography, and dance, to name a few. As a result of the theoretical frames from which it draws, this form of inquiry mandates actions that are politically committed to social justice and righting inequities in society. While there is no prescribed method for doing CAB, the types of performance selected are based on their "power to inform" (Finley, 2008, p. 143).

In our own work (Sailors & Samati, 2014), we partnered with a nonprofit nongovernmental organization in Malawi, called CRECCOM, as part of our community-based efforts to support the implementation of a national reading program. In their work, CRECCOM relied heavily on what they called Theatre for Development (emanating from Boal's 1985 work in Theatre of the Oppressed). CRECCOM conducted informal interviews and observations that led to the identification of strengths within communities to support the initiative as well as aspects that might hinder its success. CRECCOM worked with the communities to develop plays that community members performed using a participatory approach. Throughout the performance of the plays, community members commented on the issues depicted and actively worked to solve the problems. Ultimately, the community members devised an action plan for how they might minimize hindrances. This participatory and transformative approach promoted the success of the program (Sailors & Samati, 2014).

Critical arts-based methods will work well in a practice-based research project where teachers and youth work to identify challenges they face, the social structures that demand the maintenance of those challenges (as a way of keeping people "in their place"), and creative solutions to dismantle those challenges. Products such as photography and videography are widely supported through various applications that teachers and youth can use as collaborators in this process.

Pause and Reflect

If your practice-based research project draws from traditions of the post-positivist perspective, what type of analysis might support you in answering your research questions? From the interpretivist perspective? From the transformative perspective? What role do the young people in your classroom play in data analysis?

Summary

We understand that this chapter might be a bit overwhelming in the concepts presented, and it still only represents a starting point to consider options. Most researchers develop a set of tools that they continue to rely on in their research. Experience with these approaches

Points to (Re)Consider

What theory will guide your practice-based research? How will you collect your data? What analytic tools will you use to analyze your data? How will you establish credibility of your work?

builds confidence and expertise. In growing our use of the tools in this chapter, we have found it helpful to (a) find a study that uses these tools and consider it a mentor text, (b) talk with colleagues about these tools and how we are using them, and (c) use them!

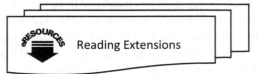

Reading Extensions

References

Albers, P., Holbrook, T., & Flint, A. (2013). *New methods of literacy research*. New York, NY: Routledge.

Boal, A. (1985). *Theatre of the oppressed* (C. A. McBride & M. L. McBride, Trans.). New York, NY: Theatre Communications Group.

Bucholtz, M. (2000). The politics of transcription. *Journal of Pragmatics, 32*, 1439–1465.

Clandinin, D. J., & Caine, V. (2008). Narrative inquiry. In L. M. Given (Ed.), *The Sage encyclopedia of qualitative research methods* (pp. 541–544). Los Angeles, CA: Sage.

DeCuir-Gunby, J. T., Chapman, T. K., & Schutz, P. A. (eds.). (2018). *Understanding critical race research methods and methodologies: Lessons from the field*. New York, NY: Routledge.

Duke, N., & Mallette, M. H. (2011). *Literacy research methodologies*. New York, NY: Guilford Press.

Finley, S. (2008). Critical arts-based inquiry. In L. M. Given (Ed.), *The Sage encyclopedia of qualitative research methods* (pp. 142–145). Los Angeles, CA: Sage.

Flanders, N. A. (1970). *Analyzing teaching behavior*. Reading, MA: Addison-Wesley Publishing Co.

Hoffman, J. V., Wilson, M., Martinez, R., & Sailors, M. (2011). Content analysis in literacy research: The past, present and future. In N. K. Duke & M. H. Mallette (Eds.), *Literacy research methodologies* (2nd ed., pp. 28–49). New York, NY: Guilford Press.

McKenna, M. C., & Kear, D. K. (1990). Measuring attitude toward reading: A new tool for teachers. *The Reading Teacher, 43*(9), 626–639.

Mertens, D. (2009). *Transformative research and evaluation*. New York, NY: Guilford Press.

Reznitskaya, A. (2012). Dialogic teaching: Rethinking language use during literature discussions. *The Reading Teacher, 65*(7), 446–456.

Riessman, C. R. (2008). Narrative analysis. In L. M. Given (Ed.), *The Sage encyclopedia of qualitative research methods* (pp. 539–540). Los Angeles, CA: Sage.

Sailors, M., & Hoffman, J. V. (2014). Establishing a print-rich classroom and school environment. In R. M. Bean & A. S. Dagen (Eds.), *Best practices of literacy leaders in schools* (pp. 184–205). New York, NY: Guilford Press.

Sailors, M., & Samati, M. (2014). Community mobilization: Supporting the implementation of a complementary reading program in Malawi. In *63rd yearbook of the Literacy Research Association* (pp. 158–171). Altamonte Springs, FL: Literacy Research Association.

Unrau, N. J., Alvermann, D. E., & Sailors, M. (2019). Literacy and their investigations through theories and models. In D. E. Alvermann, N. J. Unrau, M. Sailors, & R. Ruddell (Eds.), *Theoretical models and processes of literacy* (7th ed., pp. 3–34). New York, NY: Routledge.

Weninger, C. (2008). Critical discourse analysis. In L. M. Given (Ed.), *The Sage encyclopedia of qualitative research methods* (pp. 145–148). Los Angeles, CA: Sage.

11

Sharing Your Work With Others

Preview: In this chapter, we discuss ways in which you might share your research. We focus on ways you might share with people inside your immediate circles—including your colleagues and school and district leaders—and with larger groups of people in the field of education. We discuss the various venues that practice-based research often finds itself in.

We are literacy educators. We know the writing cycle and we are familiar with the publishing stage. We have seen the students in our classrooms as they are, at the same time, both terrified and energized with the opportunity to present their work to an audience. A writer doesn't just want to write. A writer wants to be read. A writer wants their work to be noticed and appreciated. It's not, although it may be, about wealth and fame but rather the desire to connect. Through the publishing process, the writer experiences both critique and adulation.

Points to Consider

What responsibility do you have in sharing your work? What goals do you hope to accomplish through sharing your work?

The writer is motivated to carry on and refine the craft in future endeavors.

It is no different for researchers. Presenting and publishing work is necessary not just to become part of but to grow a community of practice. This may not mean becoming famous or regarded as a rock star at conferences. For every name you recognize at a conference you attend, there are hundreds if not thousands of other professionals engaged in making research a critical part of our practice. Our goal in promoting practice-based research is to expand the circle of participants from a few hundred or a few thousand to hundreds of thousands of active researchers. Our goal in promoting practice-based research is to de-normalize research as something that university faculty do and create a new normal where educational researchers are not bounded by the context of higher education but are found everywhere there is practice.

We would disrupt the notion that there are university-based researchers who are the producers of knowledge—knowledge that is taken into practice with the teacher framed as the consumer. How can we reframe spaces (like conferences) where practice-based researchers hold similar status to university-based researchers? This is no easy accomplishment. In fact, we predict there will be resistance to this movement to broaden participation as researchers. Might such a move threaten the established norms and institutions? Quite likely, we suspect. It will be necessary for you to become not only a researcher but an activist in promoting the importance of your work—and that of your colleagues—to the field. No new order is achieved without a struggle.

In the next section, we explore traditional outlets for publishing or sharing your educational research and then explore the affordances of the 21st century in our quest to share our research.

Pause and Reflect

How can we gain access to systems that have been historically established to be exclusive? How can our practice-based research work become part of larger conversations?

Distributing Your Research: Engaging With Your Inner Circle

We recently organized and facilitated a professional writing retreat with a group of teachers. In our earliest conversations with teachers about their focus for their writing at the retreat, one teacher confessed that she had a story that was begging to share itself—the story of how she wants people to ask her not, "What are you?" (she is a person with a multiracial background) but "Who are you?" As one of the most widely read teachers we know, she started to write her story as it was important to her to write about her background, especially given that she has seen a marked increase in the numbers of children enrolling at her school who also draw from a multiracial background. Parallel to this, she was also playing around with the conundrum that her (very large) district had recently adopted a "workshop" model for the entire district. While she was excited about this, she, along with her colleagues at the retreat, recognized that many teachers neither perceived nor identified themselves as writers. Knowing what she wanted to write about but not knowing what the outlet, or venue, for her work would be, she began to play around with the idea of petitioning her school district to allow her to create a space in the district's weekly newsletter where she could "tell her story." In her telling of her story, she argued, she would be able not only to reflect on her experiences as a woman with a multiracial background but also to provide awareness of the challenges that school systems place on people like her. Similarly, she would model for other teachers in the district what it means (and looks like/sounds like/feels like) to be a writer, even as they are learning to grow their practices as writing teachers.

But, writing for the school or district newsletter is not the only way to engage your colleagues in your research. What if we used our radical imagination to plan and design other local venues for teachers to engage in conversations about their research? For example, what might it look like if schools (or districts) created spaces where practice-based research was highlighted in something akin to a "showcase of practice"? Such an event would bring teachers together in one space in a poster-like session (think science fair for teachers) where youth and their teachers would be available to talk about their classroom-based research with other teachers, other youth, and their community. Activities such as this would send very clear messages to district leaders, community members, and other teachers: We value the knowledge that teachers are creating about their practice. From the perspective of distribution and exchange, activities such as this create spaces where the exchange of knowledge about literacy teaching and learning are unavoidable. Similarly, what if those poster presentations were digitized and made widely available so that the larger community (e.g., region and state) might be able to see what teachers are doing in their classrooms, how they are studying it, and how they talk about it?

Expanding the Circle: The Worlds of Conferences and Educational Publications

While local dissemination of practice-based research is to be celebrated, we feel teachers who engage in practice-based research have an ethical and moral obligation to share their research with a wider audience and become part of a larger, professional, ongoing conversation about literacy teaching and learning and social issues. But, how do researchers go about selecting a venue for the distribution of their work? While we have organized this section dichotomously, describing conferences and publication, the two often work in conjunction with each other as part of the dissemination process. We initially discuss each separately but then attempt to bring them back together at the end of this section.

Disseminating Practice-Based Research at Conferences

Conferences play a large role in the consumption, distribution, and exchange of research and in the production of ideas for new research. They are excellent opportunities to engage in professional networks and rejuvenate intellectually. There are many different conferences that a teacher might attend. Historically, there are two types of conferences: practitioner and research. Practitioner conferences were organized to bring teachers together (the two most widely attended by literacy teachers are the annual meetings of the International Literacy Association, or ILA, and the National Council of Teachers of English, or NCTE). These practitioner conferences are held once a year in a city large enough to accommodate several thousand teachers at one time. These conferences usually take place over a three- to five-day period; teachers have the opportunity to attend both keynote sessions (think "big names") as well as smaller sessions where teachers (and teacher educators) talk about what they are doing in their classrooms. Most practitioner conferences tend to focus on pedagogies and practice. While most of these conferences are organized by professional management organizations, the Teachers for Social Justice conference is organized by teachers, for teachers. Held in San Francisco, this conference has been an annual event for quite some time. When we last went, there were over 2,000 teachers in attendance. The venue, Mission High School, is an ideal setting for a conference with political overtones, organized by teachers who care deeply about the youth with whom they work, their profession, and their community.

Other conferences historically have been organized to bring educational researchers together. In the case of literacy research, one might find literacy researchers attending the annual meetings of the Literacy Research Association (LRA) or the American Educational Research Association (AERA). These conferences also usually take place over a three- to five-day period; educational researchers have the opportunity to attend both keynote sessions (continue to think "big names") as well as smaller sessions where other researchers present their research. While these conferences vary in size (from just over a thousand at LRA to tens of thousands at AERA), their goals and purposes have historically been very different from those of practitioner conferences: Most research conferences tend to focus on research and research methods. Professional management companies organize nearly all educational research conferences.

Pause and Reflect

What type of conferences have you attended in the past? Why? Why do you think there are two distinct types of conferences? What are the political and historical reasons they are separate? Where do you think you might find practice-based research located historically? Why? What would it look like for practice-based research to cross over to research conferences?

Finding Your Community

So, you've made the decision to disseminate your research at a conference. How do you decide which conference to attend? Maybe you are already attending an annual meeting (of ILA or NCTE, for example) and want to jump in and present your work at the next meeting. If that's the case, you can skip to the next section. If you've never attended a conference, then you'll want to take a careful look at all your options and select the one that best fits the kind of work you completed in your practice-based research.

Whether you attend the large research conferences or practitioner conferences, we hope you do not underestimate the influence your research will have on the topic you studied and on the field of educational research as well. As more and more teachers present their work at conferences, more and more teachers will begin to be the very "big names" we wrote about at the beginning of this chapter.

Proposing Your Study to the Community

Now that you've identified a conference venue, you'll need to convince a panel of peers that your study is valuable and will contribute to the knowledge of others at the conference. Often, conferences receive more proposals for presentations than they can accommodate in the program; conference organizers have to make difficult decisions. How can you write a proposal for a presentation that gets selected? We have found there are a few things to think about as you prepare your conference proposal. First, read the call for proposals carefully. Focus your attention on the sections that are required and address them. Write in a way that is clear and concise (as you'll probably have a word limit). Make sure your proposal explicitly connects to the theme of the conference. Finally, check your proposal for grammatical and spelling regularity. And—it probably goes without saying—you'll want to make sure you submit the proposal before the deadline.

Presenting Your Work to Your Community: Norms and Expectations

Our presumption is that your conference proposal will be accepted. Now it's time to take your practice-based, local poster presentation and turn it into a 20-minute conference presentation. The best way to know what people who attend your session will expect from you as a presenter is to attend the conference and watch other presentations. But, if you are presenting at a conference that you are also attending for the first time, then there are a few general norms to keep in mind. These are based on having 20 minutes for your presentation. To prepare for your presentation, you probably will want to create a visual to accompany it, but avoid the dreaded "death by PowerPoint." Many people use a presentation tool (such as Keynote, Google Slides, or PowerPoint) to support them. Be aware of the colors you choose for the background and the text (e.g., yellow text is generally not a good idea). Be cognizant of too much text on a slide. And, please be aware that fancy slide transitions can distract from your message.

While the content of your slides may vary based on the expectations of your community, you might consider following the same outline used to present your written study (see the next section, "Publishing Practice-Based Research"). Certain headings (*Purpose*, *Research Question*, *Methods*, *Findings*, and *Discussion*) are common to research presentations and are largely organizational in nature. To make your presentation come to life, you'll want to include images and video where you can, without violating the confidentiality of the people who participated in your study with you—your children and youth. Strong visuals like charts and tables allow you to convey data quickly and make points effectively. You might consider practicing your presentation before you go if it is your first one. You'd be surprised how quickly time flies, and if you're not careful, you'll only be two-thirds of the way through when the timekeeper calls "time" on you!

Engaging in Research with Children and Youth

What are the parallels to research dissemination when working with youth? How can we create spaces where they are engaged as experts in what they do?

During your presentation, be aware of your timing and your time. You'll also want to be sure that you project your voice if you do not have a microphone. Rather than having people simply sit and passively receive your study, try to engage your audience in your presentation. One option is to use a Twitter feed with a hashtag as a back channel. Similarly, presentations are often organized so that there is time for questions and answers. If it is not already built in, you may want to make sure your attendees have an opportunity to ask you questions. Finally, if you are a blogger or have a space where you can interact with others, be sure you share that with your audience. Often we come away from conferences with new people to follow on Twitter and Instagram as a result of the sessions we attend.

Getting Feedback From Your Community

Conferences are an outstanding venue for distributing your research, for using it to create networks, and for using the question-and-answer session to get feedback on your work. We often find ourselves frantically jotting notes during the question-and-answer session; we use those notes to revise our work as these questions help us anticipate what we might be asked by reviewers when our work is submitted to a journal for publication (see the next section, on publishing).

Publishing Practice-Based Research

Often (but not always), people move their research from a presentation to a written report that is submitted for publication in one of the outlets we just discussed. This is not always true, but we commonly find the feedback we receive at conferences—including questions that people ask, insights that they share about their own work, and suggestions for other ways of thinking about our work—are incredibly helpful in preparing for the next step: writing a research report and submitting it for publication. In many ways, publications or articles play a more stable role in the consumption, distribution, and exchange of research than do conferences. We hope that you are considering publishing your research as a way to contribute to the larger conversation about literacy, literacy teaching, and literacy research.

There are a few things to consider in the publication process, including which journals are most appropriate for your work, how to situate your work within the larger community of practice-based and traditional research, the norms and conventions of publishing research, and getting feedback from your community. We move through each of these topics in turn in the following.

Traditional Research Journals

Research journals typically publish research reports. In this section, we want to encourage you to consider both types of research journals for your work: journals that publish practice-based research reports and ones that publish traditional research reports. Journals like *Reading Research Quarterly*, *Journal of Literacy Research*, and *Research in the Teaching of English* have historically been considered the most prestigious journals in which to publish and have (again, historically) been monopolized by university-based researchers. This is not to say the journals are not publishing empirical studies that are grounded in the everyday lives of teachers and young people. They are. But, to be published in journals like these is to follow very stringent requirements for rigor. These requirements often marginalize practice-based research. It is rare to find a practice-based study in one of these journals.

Journals Friendly to Practice-Based Research

Over the past few decades, there has been a growing recognition of the role of practice-based research, and there are now many outlets that support the distribution of research conducted by teachers like you in classrooms like yours. Figure 11.1 contains a list of the journals that (as of the publication of this book) are friendly to practice-based research.

Some of these journals are dedicated to practice-based research in its varied instantiations, including action research and teacher research; these include *Action Research*, *Educational Action Research*, and *Journal of Teacher Action Research*. Some of them are housed in countries other than the United States, such as the *Canadian Journal for Teacher Research* and the *Scandinavian Journal of Educational Research*. Others are considered practitioner journals but still publish research studies, such as the *Reading Teacher*, *Language Arts*, and the *Journal of Adolescent and Adult Literacy*. Many of the requirements of these journals mirror the expectations of

- Action Research (https://journals.sagepub.com/home/arj)
- Canadian Journal for Teacher Research (https://www.teacherresearch.ca/)
- Educational Action Research (https://www.tandfonline.com/loi/reac20)
- Educational Forum (https://www.tandfonline.com/loi/utef20)
- Journal of Inquiry and Action in Education
  (https://digitalcommons.buffalostate.edu/jiae/)
- Journal of Practitioner Research (https://scholarcommons.usf.edu/jpr/)
- Journal of Research in Education (https://journals.sagepub.com/home/rie)
- Journal of Teacher Action Research (http://www.practicalteacherresearch.com/)
- Language Arts (https://www2.ncte.org/resources/journals/language-arts/current-issue/)
- Networks: An Online Journal for Teacher Research
  (https://newprairiepress.org/networks/)
- Scandinavian Journal of Educational Research (https://www.tandfonline.com/loi/csje20)
- The New Educator (https://www.tandfonline.com/loi/utne20)
- The Reading Teacher (https://ila.onlinelibrary.wiley.com/journal/19362714/)
- Voices of Practitioners (https://www.naeyc.org/resources/pubs/vop)

FIGURE 11.1 Journals That Are Friendly to Practice-Based Research

traditional research journals, such as requirements for rigor; we provide an overview of these typical requirements in the sections that follow.

State and University-Based Journals

Many state reading and literacy associations provide space for members (and nonmembers) to publish in their regular journals. Many of these journals are issued on a quarterly basis. Figure 11.2 lists some state journals and the URL that contains directions for authors.

Some institutes of higher education also house publication outlets that are friendly to practice-based research. Figure 11.3 lists some of them and the website where they are located.

Situating Your Work Within the Community

With all the choices for where to submit your research, you might consider which journal is publishing studies similar to the one you did. We do not mean to imply that there must exist a study just like yours in the journal you choose, but you will be hard-pressed to convince an editor to publish your study if it does not easily "map onto" other studies in the journal. We like to think of finding a home (journal) for each of our studies in terms of how well the study we are preparing to submit might be considered part of an ongoing discussion within a journal. More specifically, if there is not a study in a journal that we are considering that we can cite in our own study, then the journal probably is not the best fit for our work. You might take this same stance toward finding a home (journal) for your work.

Presenting Your Work to Your Community: Norms and Expectations

In the earlier section that carries this same subtitle, we wrote about the norms and conventions of presenting your work from an oral presentation perspective. This section is about the norms and expectations for writing from an editor's perspective. Our shared experiences as past editors of research journals (Jim as past editor of *Reading Research Quarterly* and Misty as past editor of the *Journal of Literacy Research*) have given us a unique perspective on the

State organization	Publication name	Website
Alabama Literacy Association	*The Reading Paradigm*	https://www.alabamareading.org/the-reading-paradigm/
California Association of Teachers of English	*California English*	https://cateweb.org/california-english/
California Reading Association	*The California Reader*	http://californiareading.org/TCRdisplay.asp?p=TCRhome
Colorado Language Arts Society	*Statement*	https://sites.google.com/site/cololangarts/publications?authuser=0
Connecticut Reading Association	*Connecticut Reading Association Journal*	http://ctreading.org/craj/
Florida Council of Teachers of English	*Florida English Journal*	http://fcte.org/
Georgia Association of Literacy Advocates	*Georgia Journal of Reading*	http://www.georgiareading.org/journal.html
Georgia Council of Teachers of English	*Connections*	https://gcte.wildapricot.org/Connections
Illinois Association of Teachers of English	*Illinois English Bulletin*	https://iateonline.org/iate-publications/illinois-english-bulletin/
Illinois Reading Council	*Illinois Reading Council Journal*	http://www.illinoisreadingcouncil.org/publicationsservices/ircjournal.html
Indiana State Literacy Association	*Indiana Literacy Journal*	http://www.indianareads.org/journal.html
Kansas Association of Teachers of English	*Voices of Kansas*	https://www.kansasenglish.org/voices-of-kansas.html
Kentucky Council of Teachers of English Language Arts	*Kentucky English Bulletin*	https://kcte.org/publication/kentucky-english-bulletin/
Kentucky Reading Association	*Kentucky Reading Journal*	https://www.kyreading.org/resources/publications
Keystone State Reading Association	*Pennsylvania Reads*	http://ksrapa.org/membership/pennsylvania-reads/
Louisiana Reading Association	*READ: Reading, Exploration, and Discovery*	http://lareading.org/resources/publications/
State of Maryland International Reading Association Council	*Literacy Issues & Practices*	https://somiracjournal.weebly.com/read-the-journal.html
Michigan Council of Teachers of English	*Language Arts Journal of Michigan*	https://mymcte.org/publications/
Michigan Reading Association	*Michigan Reading Journal*	https://www.michiganreading.org/resources/michigan-reading-journal
Minnesota Council of Teachers of English	*Minnesota English Journal*	https://minnesotaenglishjournalonline.org/
Missouri Literacy Association	*The Missouri Reader*	https://missourireading.org/themissourireader/

FIGURE 11.2 State Literacy Journals and Their Websites

Montana Association of Teachers of English Language Arts	*Montana English Journal*	https://www.matelamt.com/publications.html
Montana State Reading Council	*Literacy Voices*	http://www.montanareads.org/literacy-voices
New England Association of Teachers of English	*The Leaflet*	http://neate.org/page/the-leaflet
New Jersey Council of Teachers of English	*New Jersey English Journal*	https://www.njcte.org/n-j-english-journal
New Mexico Council of Teachers of English	*New Mexico English Journal*	https://www.nmcte.org/2018-new-mexico-english-journal
New Mexico International Literacy Association	*New Mexico Journal of Reading*	http://www.nmira.org/nm-journal-of-reading.html
New York State English Council	*The English Record*	https://www.nysecteach.org/publications/
New York State Reading Association	*Language and Literacy Spectrum*	https://www.nysreading.org/content/publications
North Carolina English Teachers Association	*Fringes*	http://www.ncenglishteachersassociation.org/journal/
Ohio Council of Teachers of English Language Arts	*Ohio Journal of English Language Arts*	https://www.octela.org/publications/ojela/
Oklahoma Council of Teachers of English	*Oklahoma English Journal*	http://www.okcte.org/ok-english-journal.html
Oklahoma Literacy Association	*Oklahoma Reader*	http://oklahomareadingassociation.org/oklahoma-reader
Oregon Council of Teachers of English	*Oregon English Journal*	https://oregoncouncilofteachersofenglish.wildapricot.org/Oregon-English-Journal
South Carolina Council of Teachers of English	*South Carolina English Teacher*	https://www.sccte.org/publications
South Carolina State Council of the International Reading Association	*Reading Matters*	http://www.scira.org/newsletters-publications/
Tennessee Council of Teachers of English	*Tennessee English Journal* and *Visions & Revisions*	https://tncouncilofteachersofenglish.webs.com/publications
Texas Association for Literacy Education	*Texas Journal of Literacy Education*	http://www.texasreaders.org/journal.html
Texas Council of Teachers of English Language Arts	*English in Texas*	http://www.tctela.org/english-in-texas
Utah Council of Teachers of English	*Utah English Journal*	http://ucte.info/new/utah-english-journal/
Virginia Association of Teachers of English	*Virginia English Journal*	http://vate.org/publications/virginia-english-journal/
Wisconsin Council of Teachers of English Language Arts	*The Wisconsin English Journal*	http://www.wcteonline.org/publications/the-wisconsin-english-journal/
Wisconsin State Reading Association	*WSRA Journal*	https://www.wsra.org/submit

FIGURE 11.2 (Continued)

Institute of Higher Education	Publication name	Website
Florida Atlantic University	*The Journal of Literacy and Technology*	http://www.literacyandtechnology.org/
Georgia State University	*Ubiquity: The Journal of Literature, Literacy, and the Arts*	http://ed-ubiquity.gsu.edu/wordpress/
Indiana University-Bloomington	*International Journal of Literacy, Culture, and Language Education* (formerly *Working Papers in Literacy, Culture, and Language Education*)	https://education.indiana.edu/students/graduates/program-specific/lcle/working-papers.html
University of Alabama at Birmingham	*Mid-South Literacy Journal*	https://www.uab.edu/education/mlj/
University of Georgia	*Journal of Language and Literacy Education*	http://jolle.coe.uga.edu/
University of Nebraska-Lincoln	*The Nebraska Educator*	http://digitalcommons.unl.edu/nebeducator/
Western Michigan University	*Reading Horizons*	https://wmich.edu/specialed/reading-horizons

FIGURE 11.3 Institute of Higher Education-Based Journals and Their Websites

expectations for journal submissions. Here is a list of things to keep in mind, from an editorial perspective.

- Know the journal. Know what it publishes and what it does not. In order to know the journal, it is helpful to read a few articles from the most recent issues. Journals change over time (even if ever so slightly) and because of this change, it's best to read at least a few articles with an eye toward, "Does my study read like any of these studies?"

- Look for recent studies with which to align your work. Are there any studies in the journal you are considering that you can align your work with? That extend your work? If so, cite and discuss them in your report. It might be helpful to read other studies with an eye toward, "How can mine be considered as part of ongoing conversations in this journal?"

- Ask someone to read your submission before you submit it for consideration. If you have a writer's circle, ask someone in your circle to read it, even if they have read previous renditions of it. If you are not yet part of a writer's circle, ask a colleague to read it. Be sure you tell your colleague/reader which journal you intend to submit the study to. And, if you do not belong to a writer's circle, start one!

- Prepare your submission according to the expectations of the journal. Read the section about author submission guidelines carefully. Attend to the formatting requirements of the journal. If the guidelines are not clear or if you have questions, look at the formatting of recently published articles. Be sure to remove your name and any identifying information about you before you submit. This is called *blind peer review* and is an important part of the review process.

- Follow style guides. This is the set of standards for the writing and design of your research report. Style manuals provide uniformity in design and formatting within and across disciplines. All journals will specify which style guide submitting authors should follow. The vast majority of our journal articles are presented using APA (American Psychological Association) style, although we have published using both CMS (the Chicago Manual of Style) and MLA (the Modern Language Association of America) styles. The best way to know which style you should follow is to read the "author guidelines" section of your targeted journal's website carefully. You'll also want to note that some journals have what is known as a *house style* in addition to one of the three style guidelines. If there is a house style, the specifications for that style will be listed on the journal's website.

What to Include in Your Report

Typically, a research report includes the following information. But, as we stated earlier, you will want to follow the section headings suggested (or required, in some cases) by the journal.

- Introduction: In this section, you introduce the reader to the need for your study. You might think in terms of answering questions like these: Why did you need to do your study? Why did you problematize the practice that you did? Why is this study important for the educational field to pay attention to? This is the section where you probably want to state your research question(s). The most important thing that you want your reader to take away from this section is that your study is critical to solving an educational issue and will be a valuable read.

- Literature review: Most journals require at least a brief review of the literature related to your study. A literature review situates your study within a particular body of research—the one most clearly related to the topic you are studying. The reader of your study will want to know that you have "done your homework" and that you are nestling your work within an existing body of literature. Too often we hear people say, "I'm going to study [X] because there is no research on it." We have yet to come across a topic so novel that it has not previously been researched. When you present your literature review, you will probably want to be succinct and summarize the overarching "big ideas" that previous research has found about your topic.

- Methods: This section is where you will document your context, the systematic ways in which you collected and analyzed your data, and how you used your data to inform the next actions that you took during your study. Think of this as a recipe: If others are going to emulate your practice, they must know what you did as you did it.

- Findings/Interpretations: This is where you discuss what you found in your study and the ways in which your findings influence how you continue to think about the practice you problematized in your study.

- Discussion: This is the section where you show the reader how your findings relate to previous research (e.g., How did what you found align with the work of other people?). This is also where you show the unique contributions of *your* work to the field (e.g., How does your study extend and grow previous research on your practice?).

- Implications: In this section, you will speak directly to other teachers, teacher educators, practice-based researchers, or policy makers, telling them what's important in your study and why the field should pay attention.

Getting Feedback From Your Community

Once your study has been submitted, now comes the hardest part—waiting for the reviews. The editorial team of the journal will send your piece out for review. Typically, the editors ask two or three people on their editorial review board to read your study. Your identity is not known to the reviewers, and their identity is not known to you. This is known as the blind peer review process. The reviewers will read your study and will typically take the following into consideration in their review:

- How significant the study is to the field of education: To what degree does your study contribute new understandings about your problem of practice? To what degree might other practitioners use your findings to problematize their own practices?

- How sound your research methods are: This is not about whether or not you used statistics in your analysis. Rather, this is about the degree to which you proceduralized (explained) your research methods so that someone else might replicate them if they wanted. Your focus should be not only on the cyclical nature of the process but also on clear articulation of how you analyzed your data within that process and how you used those analyses to inform your practice.

- How rigorous your study is: This is about how well the methods you applied map onto your research question(s). That is, if you were studying the ways in which your youth engaged in an activist project, your study would be deemed rigorous if you engaged them in developing the interview questions that would be used for research (in the spirit of youth participatory action research) rather than administering a survey that you found online. That's not to say that you cannot use a survey, but the tool you use must map closely onto the purposes and intentions for the research. Rigor is also considered when thinking about how deeply you analyzed your data. While cursory glances at data are appropriate for making on-the-spot decisions about instruction, those glances would not be considered rigorous research methods.

- Clarity of writing: This is about how clear you are in what you say in your research report. The goal is not to use as many multisyllabic words as you can, but to write clearly so that you reduce the workload for your reader. It is also helpful to readers for writers to use active voice, not passive voice. Writing in passive voice decreases the readability of a piece and makes it more taxing on the reader to understand. Our rule of thumb came to us from Twitter: "If you can insert 'by zombies' after the verb of the sentence, you may be writing in passive voice" (Johnson, 2012)

Once your research study has been reviewed, the editors will send you a decision letter. In their letter, they will synthesize the reviews and will include a summary of their independent reading of your submission. Their decision letter will (more than likely) have one of the following decisions:

- Accept conditionally: This decision signals that the paper is read to be accepted for publication with minor changes, which are mostly conventional in nature.

- Revise and resubmit: This decision signals that the paper is interesting and fills an educational need, but there are enough concerns from the reviewers to warrant a revision in light of their feedback. Sometimes these revisions are focused on only one section of the paper (such as the need for a more clear explanation of your methods), while other times the revisions cross sections. We are always heartened by a revise and resubmit because it means we have an additional opportunity to clarify outstanding questions raised through the review process. Although we may have felt our paper (and our thoughts as they were represented in our research report) was perfect, the review process almost always helps us clarify our thinking. Our strategy is to take a deep breath and dig back into the paper, addressing the overarching "big idea" revisions first and then the more "clean it up" revisions (e.g., conventions) later.

- Reject: This is always a difficult letter to receive and read, and we have opened many of this type of decision letter over our careers. A reject is usually a result of a mismatch between a research report and the aims or goals of a journal. Or, a study does not live up to the requirements of a journal. Or, there may be some other reason. The important thing to remember about this type of letter is that it will (almost always) be accompanied by feedback from the review process. We take the reviews and decision letter of the editor as an opportunity to improve the manuscript—we revise the manuscript based on the reviews and submit it to another journal. In some cases, we have been successful on our second attempt, while in other cases, it has taken us up to three different submissions (to different journals) before we found the right "home" for our study.

Twenty-First-Century Affordances for Discussing Practice-Based Research

We live in a time in which there are many ways to share research. In many regards, we are living in the next generation of possibilities for professional interactions between teachers, practice-based researchers, university researchers, and teacher educators. While the outlets we discuss in this section do not yield themselves to full research reports, they are great ways to not only share what you are doing in your research but also engage your audience in a digital conversation with you. Those that we list here are not a complete listing but can be seen as a starting point for the beginning of informal conversations about your work with others.

Ambient Conversations via GroupMe®

One of the many things that awes us about our graduate student cohorts is the way they use social media to support each other. They use applications such as GroupMe®, a group messenger application, to support each other during their graduate coursework and to engage in ongoing professional conversations long after graduation. Applications such as GroupMe® allow for spaces where teachers can not only stay in touch but also continue to have conversations about their research. One teacher told us that a handful of teachers found each other through their shared practice of interest during their coursework and created their own group on GroupMe®. They leaned heavily on the group while they were engaged in their initial practice-based research project in their coursework, and as the year has passed since graduation, they continue to engage each other in conversations about their ongoing research on the same and other practices. The discussions they have via this application are private and are intended to support their immediate circle. Other avenues for discussions are more public.

Blogging/Vlogging and Podcasts

While they may seem to be solitary in nature, blogs and vlogs are actually social in nature. Defined as a regularly updated website or web page, a blog is usually run by an individual and is written conversationally. Different bloggers update their blogs differently, and those updates are based on the author's topic of interest. There are many platforms that will host your blog for free, including popular sites like WordPress®, Squarespace®, and Edublogs®.

Video logs (or vlogs) are regular postings that are primarily in video form. The premise for vlogs is the same as for blogs—you will want to update your vlog on a regular basis and talk to your viewer in a conversational way. YouTube® is a popular hosting site for vlogs, as is Instagram®, but you can also post your vlogs on Facebook and Twitter.

Similar to vlogs, but minus the video, are podcasts. Podcasts are digital audio files that are made available on the Internet or for download. Most people listen to podcasts on their mobile (digital) device, but they can also be accessed by a computer. They can be recorded on a smartphone. While they do not always follow the same topic, they are perfect for reporting a practice-based research project because they are typically available as a series. Anchor® and Podbean® are popular hosting sites for podcasts.

Often, blogs, vlogs, and podcasts allow for comments by readers, which are usually found at the bottom of the host web page. We see blogs, vlogs, and podcasts as a perfect way to document and share the progression of a practice-based research project. Imagine posting on a regular basis (e.g., each weekend) about your work. The opening blog/vlog/podcast might be an overview of what you will study and why it is important to you to study it. Other weekly postings might contain updates on the various pieces of your practice-based research project. For example, you could blog/vlog/podcast the summary of the literature you are reading, akin to a conversational literature review. You could blog/vlog/podcast about your methods and your thinking about the various methodological choices you are making or have made going into the study. You could blog/vlog/podcast about the data you are collecting and analyzing. Leaving a space for your readers to comment on your work might lead to the creation of new networks of peers or new ideas about what you are doing.

Unconferences

There is a growing approach to structuring professional learning based on the needs of teachers (Hicks, Sailors, & International Literacy Association, 2018). One approach that is growing in popularity is known as *unconferences*. Unconferences are meetings of people interested in similar topics. The difference between unconferences and typical conferences, or even large group meetings, is the way in which they are structured. Unconferences are loosely structured and emphasize the informal exchange of information between participants. To that end, unconferences are participant-driven meetings—people come together around a shared topic, but the logistics of what is discussed are only agreed upon once the participants have gathered. Unconferences can be very empowering; we see them as a viable way of sharing information about your practice-based research project with other practice-based researchers and other teachers who might be interested in practice-based research. Because they provide for unfiltered exchanges of ideas, unconferences are spaces where practice-based researchers can share their expertise as well as find spaces where they can ask questions that matter to them.

Professional Learning Networks via Social Media

Twenty-first-century technologies have created spaces where teachers, practice-based researchers, university researchers, and teacher educators often find themselves interacting with each other over social media. While there are plenty of examples of social media being used to exploit situations, it has also brought together people who care deeply about children and youth, teachers, education, and our society in ways that were not possible at the turn of this century. We see social media as part of what some call *professional learning networks*. The digital technologies that support these professional learning networks allow for teachers to pursue their interactions with other professionals on their own terms (e.g., on-demand) and in informal ways. These environments can be spaces where interactions between known people take place through "chats" oriented around a hashtag. There are numerous examples of these.

Some are organized by professional organizations to celebrate national days (e.g., NCTE's #WhyIWrite), while others represent ongoing conversations (e.g., Literacy SIG of the AERA's #literacies). Still others are organized more locally by individuals within schools and school districts (e.g., Edgewood Independent School District's #EISDreads). Typically, each Twitter chat is oriented around three to five predesigned "questions," and the host presents them in turn throughout the one-hour (on average) chat. People respond to the questions and to each other's responses with both text-based responses and multimedia postings (e.g., gifs, memes, and videos).

Pause and Reflect

What makes the most sense for how you want to disseminate your practice-based research? You don't have to have only one way. Maybe you want to prioritize those avenues that allow you to share your work in both formal and informal ways. How can your network and larger community of practice-based researchers support you in "breaking into" dissemination practices?

We see social media as a perfect place to engage with others in conversations about practice-based research. The hashtag that holds these conversations together might already exist (such as #literacy, #literacyresearch, or #teacherresearch), or a new one might be formed (such as #practiceresearch or #practiceliteracyresearch). Regardless, social media becomes just one more space where people who are engaged in practice-based research can collectively share and interact with each other in ways that support our work in literacy research.

Summary

We finish this part by asking the question, "What is your obligation to share your research?" This is not a trick question. The answer is always, "We must talk about our research. We must share our research." This goes back to one of our earlier conversations about the difference between inquiry and research. Inquiry is personal. Inquiry fills a "need to know." The answer to "Why are you exploring that?" (from an inquiry perspective) might be answered by something like, "Because I found it interesting" or "So I can know more about . . ."While research also is grounded in interest and researchers also learn from their work, research is a bit bigger than something personal. It is intended to contribute to a larger conversation about a topic that impacts many children, youth, and teachers. Because of this, it is imperative that practice-based researchers talk about what they are doing and share (disseminate) their research with others: those who are also doing practice-based research, those who are interested in practice-based research, and those who have yet to have heard about practice-based research.

Points to (Re)Consider

Return to the opening scenario. Were your initial thoughts affirmed throughout this chapter? Challenged? Developed? In what ways?

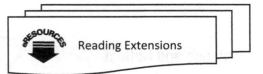

Reading Extensions

References

Hicks, T., Sailors, M., & International Literacy Association. (2018). *Democratizing professional learning for literacy educators: Empowering practices and equitable possibilities for literacy teachers*. Newark, NJ: International Literacy Association.

Johnson, R. [Johnsonr]. (2012, October 18). I finally learned how to teach my guys to ID the passive voice: If you can insert "by zombies" after the verb, you have passive voice. [Tweet]. Retrieved from https://twitter.com/johnsonr/status/259012668298506240

12 The Practice-Based Researcher
Making the Road by Walking

Preview: It's time now to stop talking the talk and to start walking the walk of a practice-based researcher. For this reason, our final chapter is the shortest in length but not the lightest in its importance to the work that lies ahead.

As literacy educators, we have worked hard over the past several decades to stop talking about reading and writing as isolated from one another and to start considering how language systems, like reading and writing, are always interacting, whether from a developmental viewpoint or from a practice perspective. It is a struggle that continues. We still see the primary curriculum, under the umbrella of literacy, divided into strands of reading and writing. We still see separate courses in many teacher preparation institutions organized around reading and writing. Dividing the two does not mean equal treatment. We continue to see that the emphasis

Points to Consider

Consider finishing this starter, "What if . . .", focusing on disrupting hegemonic practices in your classroom and school. How many of your "what if's" were centered on your practice? On actions? Which might lead to a practice-based research study?

on reading often takes precedence over an emphasis on writing in classrooms and teacher preparation, even though writing drives our society today (Brandt, 2009). Our work toward a fully integrated literacy curriculum is still in progress and is still resisted.

Is the resistance to an integrated view of literacy just a product of our roots in the field of psychology, which focused initially on reading processes and only much later on writing? Or, could there be a different explanation? Consider the fact that in Colonial America it was common to teach both White boys and White girls how to read. However, it was not common—nor was it condoned—to teach White girls to write. Writing instruction was reserved for White boys. Consider the fact that in pre-Civil War America it was encouraged to teach people who were enslaved to read, but it was strongly discouraged to teach them to write—and in fact was often prohibited by law. Even in the present, in schools that serve communities that are economically disadvantaged by social laws and practices, there is far more emphasis on reading than writing (e.g., Reading First). What is to be feared in teaching people—in particular those who are oppressed within a society—to write?

This contrast of reading and writing and the resistance to connect the two is not unlike the contrast of how researchers and practitioners are positioned. There is a strong interest in research as essential to guide practice. Indeed, evidence-based instruction is embodied in most legislation around teaching today. The presumption is that researchers develop the knowledge base that is used to tell teachers what to do (the "research into practice" mantra). Teachers are encouraged to consume research, but are they encouraged to produce research? Are they positioned as readers, not writers? The obstacles for practitioners to engage in research are many: lack of time, absence of preparation, a distraction from their role to teach, not being paid to do research, and not being needed to do research. But is there a different explanation? What are the risks associated with practitioners engaging in research? Who might be threatened? Is it possible the practice-based research could become a tool of resistance—a tool that liberates the teacher, young people, the curriculum, the community, our society? Perhaps the metaphor of choosing one path or the other is being used to divide us.

Transformation and Democratization

We recently overheard a conversation in which one teacher was talking about creating "safe spaces" for the students in her classroom. The other teacher, in response, talked about creating "brave spaces" for the students in her classroom. There is nothing safe in stepping into the transformative, practice-based researcher identity. These are brave spaces. Democracy matters in research. Voices that reflect the diversity of interests, backgrounds, and perspectives matter in research. Expect that there will be resistance within and from the established research communities. But also expect that you will find allies who are anxious to join together in a shared enterprise. Perhaps you'll be lucky enough to find an accomplice in your school, someone who collaborates with you to conspire and disrupt the hegemony that is education around the world today.

Trust the process. You have so much to offer, and the field needs to engage with your work to grow more powerful practices. Don't expect, though, that you will be met with open arms. Your work as a researcher may threaten the existing power structures and spaces for research and researchers. When you meet resistance, be prepared to argue for the importance of your work. Push, in these contexts, for the transformational. Be prepared to show and talk about the radical imagination in your work that can transform teaching literacy in schools in ways that are meaningful for all young people.

Moving Forward

We have titled this final chapter with a nod to the work of Horton and Freire (1990). The two pioneers in social reform both agreed that their work was made as they were working. The metaphor of making the road by walking it is meaningful to us because it not only represents how we view our place in the world as literacy researchers, but it also captures the essence of what it means to be a practice-based researcher. Many will rebuff us for saying this, but there is no one right way to go about living the life of a practice-based researcher. There are norms (surely) and expectations (of course) that we, as practice-based researchers, live within. And, there is a community to answer to. But, because of the transformative nature of this type of research, there is no one "right" way to do it.

What we take away from this well-loved phrase is that the road is there, before us, waiting to be made. And, it is made through praxis—reflection on what we are doing and action to change it. There are seemingly two roads being walked, one of traditional research (done by those deemed worthy of doing it) and one of the types of research we have described in this book: practice-based research. What if, rather than having two separate roads, we joined them into one? Who is being brought together as these two roads converge and for what purpose? What changes may be needed as these travelers engage with each other? How might both groups expand their perspectives, drawing on their different roots? We have seen in our work with practice-based researchers (preservice and in-service) this reverse metaphor in operation as research and practice converge into one road forward. It is not a choice between one on the other.

Some of the teachers we work with are in a place in their work with students in their classrooms where they are promoting inquiry and advocacy roles as a curricular framework. These teachers quickly pick up on the notion of practice-based research as an extension of the work they are already doing with their students. Some teachers we work with, coming at literacy instruction from a more traditional perspective, take up the practice-based researcher identity and quickly move to disrupt their own teaching into forms of literacy instruction that are more activist oriented—more about guiding their students in redesigning their world, in similar ways to the uses of research in redesigning their teaching practices.

The best time to take up practice-based research is now. There is no waiting till you start teaching, or waiting till you have years of experience. For preservice teachers and for teacher educators, we caution that viewing practice-based research as an isolated course plugged into a program will be difficult. In our program, we think of practice-based research as a part of a program that is woven together over several semesters, starting in your very first course experience. Our initial work with preservice teachers in practice-based research started with a pilot cohort. The students in this cohort became so adamant about the experience that they scheduled a meeting with the dean of the college to urge that all students in the preservice program have access to this approach. The program director only found out about this meeting after the fact, when he was called in to see the dean and met with the question: "How can we do this for everyone?" This is activism at its finest.

This same kind of advocacy stance is sweeping through our master's program as well. You start the program with a practice-based research framework, and these kinds of experiences permeate all of the courses that follow. And, while we live in the world of university-based teacher education, we know that teachers are forming learning communities (district sponsored, professional association sponsored, or independent local initiatives) that embrace practice-based research. The best time to take up practice-based research is now.

Points to (Re)Consider

How do you (now) respond to the original question we asked you: What is your identity as a researcher? What role does practice-based research play in transforming schools and society?

References

Brandt, D. (2009). *Literacy and learning: Reflections on writing, reading and society*. San Francisco, CA: Jossey-Bass.

Horton, M., & Freire, P. (1990). *We make the road by walking: Conversations on education and social change*. Philadelphia, PA: Temple University Press.

Index

Note: Page numbers in *italics* indicate figures.